AMBROSE BIERCE'S
WRITE IT RIGHT

A M B R O S E   B I E R C E ' S
WRITE IT RIGHT
. . .

The Celebrated Cynic's Language Peeves

Deciphered, Appraised, and Annotated

for 21st-Century Readers

JAN FREEMAN

WALKER

WALKER & COMPANY

NEW YORK

Published by Walker Publishing Company, Inc., New York

All papers used by Walker & Company are natural, recyclable
products made from wood grown in well-managed forests.
The manufacturing processes conform to the environmental
regulations of the country of origin.

LIBRARY OF CONGRESS CATALOGING-IN-PUBLICATION DATA

Bierce, Ambrose, 1842–1914?
    Ambrose Bierce's write it right : the celebrated cynic's
language peeves deciphered, appraised, and annotated for
21st-century readers / Ambrose Bierce and Jan Freeman.—
1st U.S. ed.
          p.   cm.
    Includes bibliographical references.
    ISBN 978-0-8027-1768-9
    1. English language—Errors of usage.   I. Freeman, Jan.
II. Title.
    PE1460.B5 2009
    428—dc22
                                                    2009019199

Visit Walker & Company's Web site at www.walkerbooks.com

First U.S. edition 2009

1 3 5 7 9 10 8 6 4 2

Designed by Simon M. Sullivan
Typeset by Westchester Book Group
Printed in the United States of America by
Quebecor World Fairfield

CONTENTS

INTRODUCTION

He would not have been contented with his legacy—he was, after all, a professional malcontent—but Ambrose Gwinett Bierce (1842–1914?) is doing pretty well in the reputation department. His most famous book, *The Devil's Dictionary*, has a fan club on Facebook, where Bierce is known as "the baddest-ass lexicographer who ever lived." Collections of his poetry, his war stories, and his supernatural yarns are available as books, DVDs, and MP3s. There are T-shirts bearing Biercean wit—*"Love, n.* A temporary insanity curable by marriage"— and even *Devil's Dictionary*–quoting boxer shorts and thongs. (Bierce would have been scandalized; he was a starchy Victorian in matters of underwear.)

Several Web sites also celebrate Bierce's work, especially his Civil War writing—both fiction and memoir—and his *Twilight Zone*–ish tales (two genres that meet in his best-known story, "An Occurrence at Owl Creek Bridge"). And Bierce remains an international man of mystery, having disappeared around the end of 1913 while he was in Mexico with Pancho Villa . . . or not.

Bierce the language maven, however, hasn't attracted much attention. This Bierce makes an appearance now and then in *The Devil's Dictionary*, where he defines *slang* as "the grunt of the human pig (*Pignoramus intolerabilis*)," and in Bierce's newspaper columns. But he didn't get a turn in the spotlight till 1909, when, at age sixty-seven, Bierce published *Write It Right: A Little Blacklist of Literary Faults*.

A career as a satirist, fabulist, and usage scourge was not an obvious future for the young Ambrose Bierce, the tenth child (of an eventual thirteen) born into a poor family in rural southern Ohio.

Bierce didn't finish high school; a year at a military academy was his most strenuous formal education. But his father had a decent library, and from boyhood Bierce was immersed in books. By the time he joined the Union army and went to war, he could produce a competent farewell sonnet for the girl he left behind.

After the war, Bierce made his way to San Francisco and found work as a journalist. He married in 1871, and spent the following three years in England with his wife, Mollie, writing for *Fun* magazine. Back in northern California, he edited and wrote for several weeklies, including the satirical *Wasp*, and eventually became a columnist for William Randolph Hearst's *San Francisco Examiner*.

The America of Bierce's lifetime was swept up in a craze for English usage books. Popular interest in language had been steadily growing throughout the 18th century, and in the 19th century the focus shifted from grammar to everyday usage advice. Thousands of Americans, both freed and unsettled by the kind of social and geographical mobility Bierce enjoyed, looked for guidance on proper speaking and writing in the shifting landscape.

Dozens of self-appointed language experts answered the call, dispensing advice in newspaper columns, periodicals, and books. Their ranks included classically educated archbishops, hardworking publishers and editors, speech coaches and schoolmasters, professors and private scholars; anyone who could find a publisher felt competent to instruct someone else, somewhere, on English usage.

The arguments could be fierce; the more scholarly authors, showing off their Greek and Latin, rained invective on their rivals in book-length debates. George Washington Moon wrote *The Dean's English* solely to rebut Henry Alford's *The Queen's English*. Fitzedward Hall's *Recent Exemplifications of False Philology* was a critique of Richard Grant White's popular *Words and Their Uses, Past and Present*.

A different type of usage book, aimed at a less sophisticated audience, also appeared in the middle of the 19th century. Walton Burgess's 1855 compendium, *Five Hundred Mistakes of Daily Occurrence in Speaking, Pronouncing, and Writing the English Language, Corrected*, may have been the first of these lists of usage errors. Burgess explained that his book was not a learned work; it was meant for those "persons—numbered by multitudes in even the most intelligent and refined communities—who from deficiency of education, or from carelessness of manner, are in the habit of misusing many of the most common words." Burgess's book might have been a bestseller, had he only thought to alphabetize his entries instead of printing them in random order.

Newspaper editors also had language preferences, but they, like Burgess's readers, had no time for theorizing. William Cullen Bryant, in 1870, made a list—an *Index Expurgatorius*, he called it—of words not allowed in the *New York Evening Post*, where he was editor. No *commence* or *compete*, no *lengthy* or *leniency* shall appear in these pages, he said; even *taboo* was taboo.

Bierce's *Write It Right*, published some forty years later, was more comprehensive than Bryant's list. But like many others of its time—and our time—it amounted to a slightly expanded version of the "bad words" collection, meant to instruct readers not just on errors but on taste. Don't use slang (*bogus, brainy*), or pretentious words (*banquet, demise*), or euphemisms (*casket, retire* for "go to bed"). When Bierce does try to justify his positions, the results aren't always pretty; he goes into stupefying detail about the difference between *necessities* and *necessaries*, for instance, and tries to explain *will* and *shall* to an increasingly indifferent audience. But he is always recognizably Bierce, dismissing the words he likes least with terse contempt: "Vulgar." "Mere slang." "Tiresome exceedingly." "Bastard forms."

I first encountered *Write It Right* in the back pages of Theodore Bernstein's 1971 usage book, *Miss Thistlebottom's Hobgoblins*, where Bierce's little blacklist is reprinted as an appendix. In my copyediting days, I would dip into it now and then, more for entertainment than for guidance. A fair number of the topics were still-familiar stylebook entries—*literally* for *figuratively*, *less* vs. *fewer*, *over* and *more than*—but many more were baffling. Why was the term *landed estate* "dreadful"? What was wrong with "I'm afraid it will rain"? Did other critics think "spend the summer" was bad English? Or "quit smoking," or "it was a success"?

In 1997, I began writing "The Word," a weekly column about English usage, for the *Boston Globe*, and now I had an excuse to dig around in the history of usage. I began to learn how many of the rules we take as gospel are actually quite recent, or are based on misunderstandings, or are simply the fossilized remains of a casual opinion delivered centuries ago. An investigation of Bierce's stylebook, as it approached its hundredth birthday, seemed like a logical entry point for a closer look at the usage faith of our forebears.

In some respects, it turns out, *Write It Right* is just like a modern usage book; it offers the conventional wisdom (surely we can figure out *lay* and *lie* if we all really try!), cautions against too-hasty innovation, warns against déclassé expressions, explains an etymology here and there.

There are differences in emphasis, however. Bierce and his contemporaries were much more hostile to slang than today's usage critics; the Victorians still imagined they could stop the surge of youthful neologizing. Like 21st-century usagists, the critics of Bierce's time disdained commercial jargon, but their animus ran deeper than ours. We might complain that *drill down* or *proactive* is clunky or needless; for them, commercial language was tainted by a long history of English snobbery toward people who earned a living by trade or manufacturing. Bierce is especially sensitive to money-related language; he invented reasons to dislike even "pay a visit" and "spend time."

And the American usagists had one handicap that burdens us no more: status anxiety about the American language. Bierce and his fellows condemned a number of words on suspicion (often incorrect) of native origin. Though earlier language mavens, notably Noah Webster, had valiantly defended our right to our own idiom, by the later 19th century many educated Americans worried that their native locutions were less refined than whatever the Brits were saying.

Bierce was no sheeplike follower, however. He may have been a stickler, but a surprising number of his sticklerish points are his own inventions. Nobody else (so far as I could find) objected to *negotiate, preparedness, as for* (instead of *as to*), or the verbs *stand* (endure) and *stand for*. We all have words we hate, of course, but today's usage critics generally resist treating their idiosyncratic peeves as universal rules. Bierce, however, had parlayed his prejudices into a successful career; he would have seen no reason to censor himself.

Overall, though, the most striking fact about *Write It Right* is how many of its 441 cautions are obsolete. Even a usage traditionalist would agree that half of them are now either resolved (we accept "run a business") or irrelevant (do we "ride" or "drive" in a carriage?); a less conservative reader might call three fourths of them extinct. The same is true, of course, of Burgess's five hundred mistakes, Bryant's list of no-no's, and a goodly number of usage rules still in print forty years ago. And nobody is campaigning to bring back the good old days when *fix* was a slovenly word, *reliable* was ill-formed, and *pants* was vulgar.

Could it be that by the year 2109, most Americans will feel just as distant from our current quarrels over *decimate, epicenter,* and *enormity*? Of course it could. Most usage conflicts die a natural death, after all; only a few language changes even attract our notice. And we have no way of knowing which disputes will live on to plague our grandchildren, though we can sometimes spot the ones that are breathing their last.

From this perspective, we might want to ask if the passion we sometimes devote to minor points of usage—from Bierce's sentence of hanging for people who use *gubernatorial* to today's online threats of beating and strangulation for people who misplace apostrophes—is perhaps a bit excessive. Would a little more historical knowledge help us keep our cool in the face of language change? Can we understand that *incentivize* may be just the new *jeopardize*, a scapegoat for our times, and not a sign that civilization is doomed?

Bierce would have bet against it, and he probably would have won. He knew that the devil gets all the best lines, and that indignation has charms that reason can't match—as he demonstrates on every page of *Write It Right*.

J.F. (2009)

AIMS AND THE PLAN

The author's main purpose in this book is to teach precision in writing; and of good writing (which, essentially, is clear thinking made visible) precision is the point of capital concern. It is attained by choice of the word that accurately and adequately expresses what the writer has in mind, and by exclusion of that which either denotes or connotes something else. As Quintilian puts it, the writer should so write that his reader not only may, but must, understand.

Few words have more than one literal and serviceable meaning, however many metaphorical, derivative, related, or even unrelated, meanings lexicographers may think it worth while to gather from all sorts and conditions of men, with which to bloat their absurd and misleading dictionaries. This actual and serviceable meaning—not always determined by derivation, and seldom by popular usage—is the one affirmed, according to his light, by the author of this little manual of solecisms. Narrow etymons of the mere scholar and loose locutions of the ignorant are alike denied a standing.

The plan of the book is more illustrative than expository, the aim being to use the terms of etymology and syntax as little as is compatible with clarity, familiar example being more easily apprehended than technical precept. When both are employed the precept is commonly given after the example has prepared the student to apply it, not only to the matter in mind, but to similar matters not mentioned. Everything in quotation marks is to be understood as disapproved.

Not all locutions blacklisted herein are always to be reprobated as universal outlaws. Excepting in the case of capital offenders—expressions ancestrally vulgar or irreclaimably degenerate—absolute proscription is possible as to serious composition only; in other forms the writer must rely on his sense of values and the fitness of things. While it is true that some colloquialisms and, with less of license, even some slang, may be sparingly employed in light literature, for point, piquancy or any of the purposes of the skilled writer sensible to the necessity and charm of keeping at least one foot on the ground, to others the virtue of restraint may be commended as distinctly superior to the joy of indulgence.

Precision is much, but not all; some words and phrases are disallowed on the ground of taste. As there are neither standards nor arbiters of taste, the book can do little more than reflect that of its author, who is far indeed from professing impeccability. In neither taste nor precision is any man's practice a court of last appeal, for writers all, both great and small, are habitual sinners against the light; and their accuser is cheerfully aware that his own work will supply (as in making this book it has supplied) many "awful examples"—his later work less abundantly, he hopes, than his earlier. He nevertheless believes that this does not disqualify him for showing by other instances than his own how not to write. The infallible teacher is still in the forest primeval, throwing seeds to the white blackbirds.

A.B. (1909)

THE BLACKLIST

A

A for An. "A hotel." "A heroic man."* Before an unaccented aspirate use an. The contrary usage in this country comes of too strongly stressing our aspirates.

• • •

With his very first bit of advice, Bierce betrays the anxiety—shared by many of his fellow language mavens—that American usage, when it differs from the British practice, is always inferior. But in the matter of *a* and *an*, he's criticizing his countrymen for an imaginary transgression. Not only Americans, but the British, too, had been changing their pronunciation of initial *h* during the 19th century. H. W. Fowler, that titan of 20th-century usage, would soon tell his fellow Britons that to write "an humble" was pedantic and undesirable, "now that the *h* in such words is pronounced" (*Modern English Usage*, 1926). For Americans today, Bierce's "bad" examples—"a hotel" and "a heroic"—are standard; it's "an hotel" that might sound foreign or snooty or both, depending on the listener's prejudices.

Action for Act. "In wrestling, a blow is a reprehensible action." A blow is not an action but an act. An action may consist of many acts.

• • •

---

* In Bierce's entries, as he explains in his preface, "everything in quotation marks is to be understood as disapproved."

Bierce's distinction still holds, more or less, in everyday use. We speak of "random acts of kindness"—each a single gesture—and of *actions*, unfolding over time, that lead to stock market melt-downs or nuclear arms agreements. But the words are sometimes interchangeable, though Bierce wishes they weren't. What he's describing is a usage distribution—*act* is more likely to be used for a single blow, *action* for a pummeling—not a clear division.

Admission for **Admittance**. "The price of admission is one dollar."

· · ·

"The price of admission" is the usual expression today, but for Bierce it's not right; it should be *admittance*. Vizetelly 1906 set out the prevailing view: "Admittance refers to place, admission refers also to position, privilege, favor, friendship, etc. An intruder may gain admittance to the ball of a society who would not be allowed admission to its membership." *Admittance* was literal, physical; *admission* was personal, figurative.

A simple rule, if it had described reality, but it didn't. Art galleries advertised both "admittance by ticket only" and "admission from eight o'clock till dusk." There were *admission* fees for *admittance* to theaters. And other language critics offered contradictory interpretations.

In the absence of a clear guideline, like the ones distinguishing *hang* from *hung* or *farther* from *further*, the usagists had no hope of imposing order on *admission* and *admittance*; eventually, they wised up and stopped trying. There are still customary differences in the way we use the words, but turning those preferences into rules has proved to be more trouble than it's worth.

Admit for **Confess**. To admit is to concede something affirmed. An unaccused offender cannot admit his guilt.

· · ·

A thief walks into a police station. He isn't a suspect, so he can't say "I want to admit a crime," says Bierce; he can only say "I want to confess a crime."

Of course, in our noncriminal lives, we often "admit" rhetorically to imaginary accusations: "I admit, I never before considered the subtleties of *admit* and *confess*." In the literal sense, though, Bierce's distinction is fair; the question is, why does he make it? Did his fellow journalists habitually misuse *admit* for *confess*?

Other language critics said the real problem was the use of *confess* for *admit*. Raub 1897 thought that *confess* implied culpability, so it was wrong to say "I confess I thought he was the taller of the two." But he was mistaken; *confess* had been used since the 16th century, says the *Oxford English Dictionary*, to mean simply "[make] a disclosure of private feeling." See *Self-confessed*.

Adopt. "He adopted a disguise." One may adopt a child, or an opinion, but a disguise is assumed.

· · ·

To 21st-century ears this is a mysterious edict, but Frank Vizetelly, an American lexicographer and language adviser, explained the reasoning behind it in a 1922 booklet called "S.O.S—Slips of Speech." *Adopt*, said Vizetelly, implies taking over from someone else: You *adopt* a plan furnished by another, but you *choose* a plan you've come up with yourself. This suggests that you could indeed "adopt a disguise" if it already existed—your sister's hand-me-down Halloween costume, say—but Bierce didn't vex himself with such subtleties.

Advisedly for **Advertently, Intentionally.** "It was done advisedly" should mean that it was done after advice.

· · ·

Advisedly includes the word *advised*, so it must include the concept as well, says Bierce. But the *OED* gives examples of *advisedly* dating back to 1375, and in none of them does the word mean "with advice." It does have a bunch of senses that mean "as if done with [good] advice,"—that is, "cautiously, prudently, deliberately, intentionally." Maybe it should mean "done after advice," but it doesn't, and it never has.

Afford. It is not well* to say "the fact affords a reasonable presumption"; "the house afforded ample accommodation." The fact supplies a reasonable presumption. The house offered, or gave, ample accommodation.

. . .

The rest of the world, including Bierce's fellow usage writers, used *afford* to mean "supply, give, furnish." The *OED*'s earliest citation, from the 16th century, even refers (like Bierce's "bad" example) to a house: "Can a countrie cotage affoord such perfection?" But as Bierce announces in his preface, this is his book, and he will decide which is the "actual and serviceable" meaning of each word. We are left to deduce that he approves of *afford* only in the sense "be able to pay for."

Afraid. Do not say, "I am afraid it will rain." Say, I fear that it will rain.

. . .

The origin of this odd prescription is obscure; the earliest version of it I've seen is in *Five Hundred Mistakes . . . Corrected*, by Walton Burgess (1855). Mistake No. 387 is "I am *afraid* it will rain"; Burgess insisted on "I fear," because "*afraid* expresses terror; *fear* may mean only *anxiety*."

Burgess's distinction was sheer fantasy, however. The *OED* has

---

* Where Bierce writes "It is not well to say," we usually now write "It is not good." But *well* is an adjective as well as an adverb, and a century ago Bierce's expression was common: "It is well to keep these distinctions" (Fitzgerald 1901).

examples of "be afraid" meaning "expect something unpleasant" as early as 1530, and Shakespeare used it for "regretfully suspect" in *The Merchant of Venice* (1596): "I am much afraid my Ladie his mother plaid false."

Bierce was one of a very few usage critics to adopt the Burgess line; most of them, though they surely tried, just couldn't see a difference worth mentioning between "I'm afraid" and "I fear."

Afterwards for **Afterward.**

• • •

Both versions of the word are standard, though *afterwards* is more common in Britain. Historically the suffixes *-ward* and *-wards* are the same: "The choice between them is mostly determined by some notion of euphony in the particular context," says the *OED*. "Some persons, apparently, have a fixed preference for the one or the other." At American publications, the fixed preference is generally for the *s*-less versions: *afterward, backward, toward, upward,* and so on. But *afterwards* and its fellows are not incorrect; in the world not governed by publishers' stylebooks, they're just as respectable as their slightly shorter cousins.

Aggravate for **Irritate.** "He aggravated me by his insolence." To aggravate is to augment the disagreeableness of something already disagreeable, or the badness of something bad. But a person cannot be aggravated, even if disagreeable or bad. Women are singularly prone to misuse of this word.

• • •

Aggravate, from the Latin for "make heavier," was first used to mean "annoy" in 1611. That sense must have caught on in the later 1800s, for the usage arbiters began denouncing it around 1870 and kept at it for more than a century.

But if the naysayers thought they were being loyal to their Latin, they were mistaken. Even among the Romans, notes

Merriam-Webster's Dictionary of English Usage, the secondary sense of *aggravare* was "to bear down upon or annoy." Dickens and Melville and William F. Buckley Jr. used *aggravate* for "irritate," says *MWDEU*, and that meaning is widely accepted. Since there's no chance of confusing the senses—*aggravate* meaning "make worse" always has an inanimate object, while *aggravate* meaning "annoy" applies to people—the (dwindling) hostility to *aggravate* seems like mere nitpicking nostalgia.

As for Bierce's aside about women—well, maybe it's true; but then, the women of his era had more to be aggravated about than the men.

All of. "He gave all of his property." The words are contradictory: an entire thing cannot be of itself. Omit the preposition.

• • •

All of had only recently become a usage issue, and Bierce may have been following Vizetelly 1906, who used the same reasoning to demonstrate that *all of* was nonsensical: "You may say 'ship some, or any definite number, say ten of them,' or 'ship them all,' but not 'ship all of them.'" That is, you can take "some of them"—some part *of* a whole—but once you take "all," there's no "them" remaining, and so "of them" is meaningless.

Neither man mentions that Shakespeare, Addison, and Austen used *all of*, nor that Abraham Lincoln supposedly said you couldn't fool all of the people all of the time. This rule didn't fool any of the people any of the time; everybody went right on writing "all his property" or "all of his property," as idiom and rhythm demanded. People with nothing better to do may tell you that *all of* is wordy, but at least these days they won't claim that it's logically impossible.

Alleged. "The alleged murderer." One can allege a murder, but not a murderer; a crime, but not a criminal. A man that is merely suspected of crime would not, in any case, be an alleged criminal, for an allegation is a definite and positive statement. In their tiresome addiction to this use of alleged, the newspapers, though having mainly in mind the danger of libel suits, can urge in further justification the lack of any other single word that exactly expresses their meaning; but the fact that a mud-puddle supplies the shortest route is not a compelling reason for walking through it. One can go around.

· · ·

Bierce's argument against *alleged* was restated in 1965 by another newspaperman and usage critic, Theodore Bernstein, in *The Careful Writer.* "You don't allege a person, but rather a crime or a condition," Bernstein said. Phrases like "alleged spy" and "accused thief" are not parallel with "trained soldier," he cautioned, and to the reader or listener, "alleged spy" may sound like a kind of spy, not a person accused of spying.

In fact, though, as Bernstein conceded, there's no grammatical flaw in such expressions, any more than in "presumed winner" or "supposed leader." The news media often choose to avoid such modifiers in crime stories, but it's a matter of journalistic courtesy, not grammar.

Allow for **Permit**. "I allow you to go." Precision is better attained by saying permit, for allow has other meanings.

· · ·

Vizetelly 1906 explained the usual distinction: "One *allows* that to which one interposes no objection," while "one *permits* that to which one gives express consent." Not every situation is clearly in one category or the other, however, and writers have plenty of leeway. "*Permit* is often used as a synonym of *allow*, but it has a connotation of more formality in the authorization," said Evans and Evans 1957, and the level of formality is often a matter for the writer's judgment.

Allude to for **Mention.** What is alluded to is not mentioned, but referred to indirectly. Originally, the word implied a playful, or sportive, reference. That meaning is gone out of it.

· · ·

The idea of restricting *allude* to the most delicate, indirect sorts of reference was new, and Alfred Ayres, in *The Verbalist* (1881), made it clear that the practice was otherwise: "*Allude* is now very rarely used in any other sense than that of to speak of, to mention, to name." Ayres called that a "degradation"—he thought *allude* should walk the fine line between the more explicit *refer* and the more discreet *hint*—but the looser usage, like the "correct" one, was more than three hundred years old.

Not everyone signed on to the new rule. In *Slips of Tongue and Pen* (1889), J. H. Long treated *allude* and *refer* as synonymous: "The real meaning of *allude or refer to* is to touch lightly upon, to call attention to, delicately or indirectly." So did Joseph Fitzgerald, in *Word and Phrase* (1901): "These two verbs . . . both denote passing attention to some matter, never anything like discussion of it, study of it, weighing of it." But many commentators spent pages debating just how indirect a proper allusion had to be.

Usage books and dictionaries still mention the narrow sense of *allude*, but it is rarely enforced. And while Garner 2003 points out that the phrase "allude explicitly" is weird, few other uses would raise eyebrows.

And so. And yet. "And so they were married." "And yet a woman." Omit the conjunction.

· · ·

What could be bothering Bierce here, and which conjunction does he want us to omit? It doesn't matter: This is balderdash, piffle, and bunkum. There is nothing wrong with "and so" or "and yet."

William Strunk Jr., the Cornell English professor, had not yet published his battle cry, "Omit needless words!"; that would come in 1918, in the original *Elements of Style*. But Bierce's injunction seems to spring from the same idea—no doubt a journalistic axiom when he became a newspaperman—that anything omittable should be omitted. Bierce should have read more bedtime stories to his children; he would have known that "And so they were married" is not the same as plain "So they were married."

And which. And who. These forms are incorrect unless the relative pronoun has been used previously in the sentence. "The colt, spirited and strong, and which was unbroken, escaped from the pasture." "John Smith, one of our leading merchants, and who fell from a window yesterday, died this morning." Omit the conjunction.

. . .

Perhaps this construction was more common in the 19th century— several other usage writers caution against it—but today, it doesn't make anyone's list of Top 100 usage gaffes.

Antecedents for **Personal History**. Antecedents are predecessors.

. . .

The usage Bierce is condemning is the fashion, then recently borrowed from the French, of using *antecedents* for a person's curriculum vitae. White 1870 had been more forceful: "To call the course of a man's life until the present moment *his antecedents* is nearly as absurd a misuse of language as can be compassed . . . Ask instead 'What do you know of his previous life?'"

It was then correct, however, to use *antecedents* to mean one's predecessors in office: "The *antecedents* of President Arthur are the Presidents from Washington down" (Fallows 1885). Both these senses have since been supplanted by one that was not even on the horizon a century ago: *antecedents* meaning "forebears" or "ancestors."

Anticipate for Expect. "I anticipate trouble." To anticipate is to act on an expectation in a way to promote or forestall the event expected.

. . .

To *anticipate* an event, the purists said, was to do something about it, not just wait for it. Of course, it's hard to tell what constitutes an act: We might argue that mental preparation should count as "anticipation." Today's style mavens still caution against using *anticipate* for the simpler *expect*, but *anticipate* has so many shades of meaning that a general rule is almost useless. Maybe that's why the issue no longer turns up on many pet-peeve lists.

Anxious for Eager. "I was anxious to go." Anxious should not be followed by an infinitive.* Anxiety is contemplative; eagerness, alert for action.

. . .

The *anxious-eager* distinction was brand-new in Bierce's day: It was born in 1901, when Alfred Ayres, writing in *Harper's* magazine, congratulated himself on having noticed it. (The *Bookman*, a New York literary magazine, responded with an item on Ayres's discovery headlined "Priggishness Made Perfect.")

Bierce's version of the rule—that *anxious* is "contemplative"— is a bit more obscure than the standard formulation; we usually hear that *anxious* should apply to worry and *eager* to pleasurable anticipation. But *anxious* and *eager* had already been mingling their meanings for at least two centuries, ever since Dryden, in a 1687 poem, described mankind as "anxious to reign, and restless on the throne." Despite that history, though, Ayres's version of proper usage became a classroom shibboleth, imposed on generations of young Americans.

* There's no grammatical reason to avoid using *anxious* with the infinitive. Bierce probably bans it because *anxious to* usually means "eager to," the usage he rejects.

In practice, of course, the rule is widely ignored, perhaps because it never made much sense. *Eager* and *anxious* overlap in meaning not because our speech is careless, but because eagerness and anxiety coexist in the human heart.

Appreciate for **Highly Value.** In the sense of value, it means value justly, not highly. In another and preferable sense it means to increase in value.

• • •

Appreciate was a much debated verb from the 1880s into the 1960s, though the critics never agreed on which of its several senses should be thrown overboard. Bierce's first sense, "value justly," is still familiar: "I appreciate the irony of my situation." But today we're more likely to use the verb to mean "be grateful for, value highly"—which seems fair enough, since that definition first appeared in an English dictionary in 1742.

As for the financial sense—"my stocks are appreciating"—it was a recent Americanism, and commercial as well. (It was even used transitively, said Schele de Vere 1871, as in, "These improvements will *appreciate* the farm." Shades of "growing the business"!) Ordinarily Bierce would call such a usage vulgar, but this time he approves; maybe his stocks *were* appreciating.

Approach. "The juror was approached"; that is, overtures were made to him with a view to bribing him. As there is no other single word for it, approach is made to serve, figuratively; and being graphic, it is not altogether objectionable.

• • •

Was bribing jurors so common in Bierce's time that a special euphemism was needed to describe the attempt? Maybe so, since he reluctantly accepts the usage. *Approach* still is used to mean "make an overture," but we no longer assume the overture is a criminal attempt.

Appropriated for **Took**. "He appropriated his neighbor's horse to his own use." To appropriate is to set apart, as a sum of money, for a special purpose.

· · ·

Bierce would like to restrict the verb *appropriate* to official uses, such as Congress's assignment of public funds, but the word had never observed those limits; in both legal and everyday language, it meant simply "take for oneself." His specific target, however, may have been the jocular use of *appropriate*, which was then common: "My young friend, thou art wrong, and slanderous, and presumptuous! . . . I have not stolen [a costume]; nay, verily, I have only appropriated" (Henry Peterson, *Pemberton*, 1873).

Approve of for **Approve**. There is no sense in making approve an intransitive verb.

· · ·

He's Ambrose Bierce, and he approves—not *approves of*—this message. But senselessly or not, *approve* had been used as an intransitive verb since the mid-17th century. The *OED* cites "our modern assertors and predicators approve on it" (1658) and "he has read all, but approves of very few" (1711). *Approve* without the preposition is the older form, but either version is correct.

Apt for **Likely**. "One is apt to be mistaken." Apt means facile, felicitous, ready, and the like; but even the dictionary-makers cannot persuade a person of discriminating taste to accept it as synonymous with likely.

· · ·

Actually, *apt* had been used to mean "likely" for more than three centuries before anyone raised an alarm. The *OED*'s earliest example is from Thomas More's *Heresyes* (1528): "Yet be such workes . . . apte to corrupt and infect the reder." It was only in the 19th century that usage gurus began to address the fine points of using *apt, likely,* and *liable*. "*Apt* implies natural fitness or tendency," said Vizetelly 1906; "*likely* applies to a contingent event." The distinctions are still covered in many modern guides; Garner 2003, for example, advises that "the best American usage" follows the British in using *apt* for habitual rather than particular tendencies. Bierce, however, seems to reject even these rules, insisting that *apt* is proper only in uses like "an apt pupil" and "an apt illustration." See *Liable*.

Around for **About.** "The débris of battle lay around them." "The huckster went around, crying his wares." Around carries the concept of circularity.

• • •

The use of *around* where the British would say *about* is recorded in America from Revolutionary times, but it was only in the later 19th century that critics begin to question it. Other usage writers didn't join Bierce in limiting *around* to strictly circular arrangements, but they did have their doubts about it. Maximilian Schele de Vere included *around*, in the sense of "in the neighborhood of," in *Americanisms* (1871). Utter 1916 called it not just American but "a colloquialism." But Americans went right on "standing around" and "traveling around," and not just in circles. In 1957, in *A Dictionary of Contemporary English Usage*, Bergen and Cornelia Evans declared that the use had been standard "for at least seventy-five years"—that is, since a quarter century before Bierce's futile protest.

Article. A good and useful word, but used without meaning by shopkeepers; as, "A good article of vinegar," for a good vinegar.

• • •

"Let us not forget that we can make a good article of butter right here on our farms," says the 1888 Annual Report of the Ohio State Board of Agriculture, using the language Bierce deplores. It may have been commercial jargon in some uses, but *article* had the sense "material thing" as early as 1618, and the phrase "articles of furniture" dates to 1734. The grocer no longer offers "a good article of vinegar," and "articles of furniture" are more often "items" today. But "article of clothing" is still so familiar that the *OED* found its example in a *Seinfeld* script: "Socks are the most amazing article of clothing."

As for That, or If. "I do not know as he is living." This error is not very common among those who can write at all, but one sometimes sees it in high place.

· · ·

The "don't know as" formulation was once standard English—the *OED* quotes William Caxton and Samuel Richardson using it—but by the time Bierce was learning his craft, it was regional dialect in both England and America. The standard usage, then as now, was "I do not know that he is living."

As—as for So—as. "He is not as good as she." Say, not so good. In affirmative sentences the rule is different: He is as good as she.

· · ·

Once upon a time, it was more common in English to use *so . . . as* in negative comparisons—"'Tis not so deep as a well"—and *as . . . as* in positive ones: "He's as talented as she is." That habit began to weaken a century or so before Bierce was born, and it has weakened further since he wrote. That's only natural, notes *MWDEU*, since the *so . . . as* prescription is unusual; the English language "does not in general have different grammatical structures for negative statements," so there are no parallel usages to help reinforce this one in our minds. In any case, the *so . . . as* construction has never been a really big deal; Evans and Evans 1957 recommended using it only if you wanted to intensify the negation, and these days it's a matter of style, not rule.

As for for **As to.** "As for me, I am well." Say, as to me.

. . .

Bierce seems to have been alone in this opinion, and he was swimming against the usage tide: Both before and since his pronouncement, *as for* has been more common with a personal pronoun ("As for me, I daily wished more to please him"—*Jane Eyre*). *As to* was once more usual with impersonal pronouns—"as to that"—and it's still in everyday use. But *as for* is more common overall, and universally accepted.

At Auction for **By Auction.** "The goods were sold at auction."

. . .

Seth T. Hurd, in *A Grammatical Corrector* (1847), tried to explain why *at auction* must be wrong: "The property will be sold *by* increasing the price from the lowest to the highest 'bid,' not *at* increasing it. And this is in analogy with the expressions: He was wounded *by* a shot, *at* the battle . . . The articles were sold by auction, at an auction."

British English still frequently uses *by auction,* but Americans seem to have decided to treat an auction as both an event *at* which and a means *by* which objects are sold to the public.

At for **By.** "She was shocked at his conduct." This very common solecism is without excuse.

. . .

Few other critics mentioned "shocked at," but several of Bierce's contemporaries made the same argument about "angry at," insisting that we are angry *at* a situation but angry *with* a person. Vizetelly 1906 called "angry at you" (instead of "with you") "an unpardonable vulgarism." Bierce thinks *shocked* should pair up only with *by,* and that is indeed its usual mate. But Sir Richard Steele wrote of men "shocked at Vice and Folly" in 1711, and Charlotte Brontë wrote "shocked at herself" in 1869. Even the *OED* glosses *shocked* as "scandalized or horrified *at*." It is curious that Bierce was so scandalized by, or at, the less common preposition.

Attain for **Accomplish.** "By diligence we attain our purpose." A purpose is accomplished; success is attained.

· · ·

Whatever problem Bierce perceived in the popular use of these verbs, it was not serious enough to attract the attention of other critics in his day. Half a century later, Eric Partridge mentioned the words, not very helpfully, in *Usage and Abusage*: "to *attain* is 'to reach, to gain, to achieve'; to *accomplish* is 'to perform (a task), to succeed in (an undertaking).'" There are differences, of course, but Bierce's rule wouldn't be much help to a writer with no sense of how the words are used.

Authoress. A needless word—as needless as "poetess."

· · ·

Indeed. We can only wonder if Bierce—no fan of feminism, though he liked clever women—would say the same today about *actress, waitress,* and *hostess.* See *Poetess.*

Avocation for **Vocation.** A vocation is, literally, a calling; that is, a trade or profession. An avocation is something that calls one away from it. If I say that farming is some one's avocation I mean that he practises it, not regularly, but at odd times.

· · ·

If you've known these words since high school Latin class, you'll be surprised to learn that *vocation* and *avocation* have been confused for more than two centuries. "In the best reputed Journals of the present day, the same ignorant misapplication of the term [avocation] may continually be seen," a correspondent complained to the London-based *Gentleman's Magazine* in 1826. "Why is this? Simply, because avocation is a fine-sounding word, much more shewy than business, employment, &c."

But it was not linguistic pretension that doomed *avocation* to ambiguity, the *OED*'s account suggests; it was the facts of life in the 18th century. If you had two lines of work, equally important, which was vocation and which avocation? Both words were being used for "occupation" by the mid-18th century, and the confusion has been lamented by usagists from the mid-19th century to the present.

The dictionaries, however, have conceded the point, simply giving "vocation" as one sense of *avocation*. So the usage problem is the same today as it was in 1909 (and 1809): You may use *vocation* to mean "job" and *avocation* to mean "hobby," as every language maven recommends, but you can't be sure your audience will know the difference.

Avoid for Avert. "By displaying a light the skipper avoided a collision." To avoid is to shun; the skipper could have avoided a collision only by getting out of the way.

• • •

Avoid had not been much of a usage issue in the 19th century. Ayres mentioned it, though not in contrast to *avert*, in 1896: "We often see this word, which means to shun, to keep away from, misused in the sense of prevent or hinder, thus: 'There shall be no cause of complaint if I can *avoid* it.'"

Later usage critics continued to point out that *avert* means to ward off, or turn aside, a threat, while *avoid* means to move out of its way. But it doesn't loom large as a usage problem; Garner 2003 mentions only *avert*, which he defines as "to turn away or avoid."

Avoirdupois for **Weight**. Mere slang.

. . .

Mere slang, as Bierce says, and yet it has been in use, as a jokey synonym for weight, from Shakespeare's time to our own: "The weight of a hair will turn the scales between their avoirdupois," says Falstaff of Prince Hal and Poins. The word was especially popular in Bierce's day, however, as a comic-genteel word for fat. "Lady Caroline Sellwood was honestly dishonest to the last ounce of her two hundredweight of avoirdupois," wrote Ernest W. Hornung in an 1897 novel. The title character of George Ade's *The Slim Princess* (1911) suffers from what her father considers a "pitiful shortage of avoirdupois." But whether because it was slang or because it was coyly euphemistic, *avoirdupois* was not Bierce's kind of wit.

B

Back of for **Behind, At the Back of**. "Back of law is force."

. . .

Back of, along with its sidekick *in back of*, was already a second-class citizen of the lexicon, a lowly Americanism, when Bierce declared it should be banned outright. That attack launched "a tradition of condemning these inoffensive phrases," says *MWDEU*, for a variety of invented reasons: They were "colloquial," "undesirable," "an illiteracy," "childish." By 1957, the frenzy had died down, and in *A Dictionary of Contemporary American Usage*, Bergen and Cornelia Evans said that "in back of" was now "accepted in the finest circles." Not so fast: Garner 2003 believes that "good editors tend to replace either phrase with *behind*." Shouldn't that depend on what the good editor is editing? "In back of" may be casual and American, but sometimes casual American is just the tone you want.

Backwards for **Backward**.

. . .

See *Afterward*.

Badly for **Bad**. "I feel badly." "He looks badly." The former sentence implies defective nerves of sensation, the latter, imperfect vision. Use the adjective.

. . .

The joke that "I feel badly" means your fingers aren't working was labored even in 1909, but at least it was new; it seems to have been launched by Frank Vizetelly, three years earlier, in *A Desk-Book of Errors in English*. By now, it should be long gone—after all, nobody in recorded history has ever misunderstood "I feel badly" as a statement about digital numbness—but usage commentators just can't stop repeating the whiskery witticism.

The question remains, though: Why do people who would not say "I feel sadly" nevertheless choose "I feel badly," as if *badly* were an adjective? *MWDEU* offers a number of potential reasons. There's the familiarity of other *feel*-plus-adverb combinations like "feel strongly" and "feel passionately," which are different grammatically but sound similar. There's the influence of "feel good" and "feel well": Some people use *good* for emotional states and *well* for physical condition, and "many make the same distinction with *bad* and *badly*, choosing *feel bad* for health and *feel badly* for emotion."

Still others may think of *bad* as meaning primarily "wicked." In fact, Richard Meade Bache, in his 1869 usage book *Vulgarisms*, said this was the only proper sense: "*To feel bad* is to feel conscious of depravity; to feel *badly* is to feel sick."

If Bierce checked in today, he might count this battle a victory: In print, at least, "feel badly" is a minority usage, far outstripped by "feel bad." Then again, he might be secretly pleased to find the stigmatized usage still with us, and modern grammar scolds still repeating his feeble joke about defective fingertips.

Balance for **Remainder.** "The balance of my time is given to recreation." In this sense balance is a commercial word, and relates to accounting.

· · ·

"Commercial" jargon was as unwelcome in everyday English a century ago as it is now—perhaps more so, since the English gentleman's hereditary disdain for trade still colored the language. But the everyday sense of *balance* that Bierce rejects was at least a century old in America when he wrote, and already invading British usage.

Other critics attacked it not as jargon but as inaccurate. "Balance is metaphorically the difference between two sides of an account—the amount which is necessary to make one equal to the other," said Richard Grant White in *Words and Their Uses* (1870). "It is not the rest, the remainder."

The stigma lingered well into the 20th century; as late as 1971, Theodore Bernstein, the *New York Times*'s usage maven, found *balance* "not entirely acceptable." That would soon change: Five years later, the word appeared in the *Times* under the byline of the very persnickety William F. Buckley Jr. In his review of *The Company*, by Watergate conspirator John Ehrlichman, Buckley wrote, "About the balance of the book . . . one can only say that it is so bad it might have been ghosted by John Dean." With friends like Buckley, *balance* was soon welcome even in Bernstein's world.

Banquet. A good enough word in its place, but its place is the dictionary. Say, dinner.

· · ·

Pretentiousness was the charge against *banquet*. William Cullen Bryant had banned it from the pages of the *New York Evening Post* in 1870. Vizetelly 1906 elaborated: "This word designating a sumptuous feast in honor of some person or event should not be used as the synonym of 'dinner' or 'supper.'" Emily Post, in *Etiquette* (1922), included *banquet* on a list of pretentious terms to avoid, along with *mansion* for big house, *liquid refreshment* for drink, and *ablutions* for washing. She approved *banquet*, however, to mean "a semi-public lunch or dinner" with a program or speaker—not foreseeing, perhaps, that under that definition, the soccer team's awards dinner would one day qualify as a banquet.

Bar for **Bend.** "Bar sinister." There is no such thing in heraldry as a bar sinister.

· · ·

Bierce is correct; real heraldry knows no bar sinister. A coat of arms may show a bend sinister (a band from the upper left to lower right) or a bar (parallel horizontal bands), but the bar sinister is fictional; it was created by Sir Walter Scott, in his 1823 novel *Quentin Durward*, as a symbol of bastardy.

But so what? There's no E.T., no Shangri-La, no Sherlock Holmes, and no "oil of dog"—the key ingredient in one of Bierce's best-known stories. As a fiction writer himself, Bierce might have been more sympathetic to Scott's invention.

"Bar sinister" may not exist in heraldry, but it has a rich life in language and pop culture. It served as a euphemism for illegitimacy back when such euphemisms were required: "I say, Harry, I wish thou hadst not that cursed bar sinister," says a Thackeray character. It has furnished a book title, a film title, and a band's name, as well as, most memorably, the moniker of *Underdog*'s cartoon archvillain: Simon Bar Sinister.

Because for **For.** "I knew it was night, because it was dark." "He will not go, because he is ill."

· · ·

This directive is a puzzler, because to modern ears, both of Bierce's "wrong" sentences sound acceptable. We could substitute *for* in either, as he recommends, but *for* sounds more elevated and formal now than it would have to Bierce and his contemporaries.

The words aren't always equivalent, of course. *Because* puts more emphasis on causation; we don't say "I bought it for it was so cheap" (or "For it was so cheap, I bought it"). *For*, said Webster 1913, "connects less closely [than *because*], and is sometimes used as a very general introduction to something suggested by what has gone before." But in Bierce's examples, and often in his other work, there are cases where either conjunction seems plausible. "A slight is less easily forgiven than an injury, because it implies something of contempt," he wrote. Why *because* instead of *for*?

It seems likely that this is Bierce's mania for precision at work; as he tells us in his preface, he thinks a word has but one "actual and serviceable" meaning, and if there are two words to choose between, one must be better. He may well have formulated a rule to govern his own choice between *for* and *because*; unfortunately, he doesn't tell us what it is.

Bet for **Betted.** The verb *to bet* forms its preterite regularly, as do *wet, wed, knit, quit* and others that are commonly misconjugated. It seems that we clip our short words more than we do our long.

. . .

Even in 1909, Bierce was almost alone in his insistence that *betted*, *wedded*, *wetted*, and *quitted* were the only acceptable past tenses. Theodore Bernstein, weighing in some sixty years later, observed that Bierce "has not had his way in any of these instances and is not likely to have . . . *Bet* as the past tense is far more common—and just as valid—as *betted*."

Body for **Trunk.** "The body lay here, the head there." The body is the entire physical person (as distinguished from the soul, or mind) and the head is a part of it. As distinguished from head, *trunk* may include the limbs, but anatomically it is the torso only.

• • •

Let's get this straight: The head is part of the body, says Bierce, so a headless body is not a body but a *trunk*—unless it's a limbless *torso.* Did Bierce's fellow journalists really have to make this distinction often? More likely it's his own grisly usage point, born of his vivid imagination and his Civil War service, which exposed him to body parts in all varieties of gruesomeness.

But ever since Old English, we've been using *body* to mean either the entire organism or the body as contrasted with the head. If you should ever stumble on a headless trunk and a trunkless head, the police will not misunderstand when you tell them, "The head is here and the body there."

Bogus for **Counterfeit, or False**. The word is slang; keep it out.

• • •

Bierce is so hostile to slang that he passes up the chance to tell an excellent etymological yarn. John Russell Bartlett was not so restrained; in his *Dictionary of Americanisms* (1877), he quoted an explanation from the *Boston Courier* of June 12, 1857: "The word *bogus* is a corruption of the name of one *Borghese,* a very corrupt individual, who, twenty years ago or more, did a tremendous business in the way of supplying the great West, and portions of the South-west, with counterfeit bills and bills on fictitious banks. The Western people fell into the habit of shortening the name of Borghese to that of *Bogus.*"

The tale was thoroughly bogus, but the word itself was 24-karat slang gold. The *New York Times* had been circulating *bogus* since 1858, when it published the tale of a New York cop sent to bust a dozen "bogus lottery and gift concerns" in southern New

Hampshire. *Harper's* and the *Atlantic* picked up *bogus* in the 1860s. Bryant 1870 put it on his list of banned words, but he was too late. By the time Bierce made his appeal, nearly forty years after Bryant, there was no way to "keep it out"; *bogus* was already in.

Both. This word is frequently misplaced; as, "A large mob, both of men and women." Say, of both men and women.

· · ·

Bierce's advice on parallel construction is traditional and unobjectionable, though you might prefer, like Fowler 1926, to write "both of men and of women." But it's a minor issue; most people wouldn't notice either way, any more than they notice those allegedly misplaced *only*s. (And in another mood, Bierce might have recommended another solution: Why not say simply "a large mob of men and women"?) See *Only*.

Both alike. "They are both alike." Say, they are alike. One of them could not be alike.

· · ·

Since the 18th century, usage writers have enjoyed bashing *both alike* (and *both agree* and *both together*) as redundant. Yes, Shakespeare wrote of "two households, both alike in dignity, In fair Verona"; the King James Version of Psalm 139 has "The darkness and the light are both alike to Thee." And Henry Alford, dean of Canterbury and author of *The Queen's English*, preached in 1856 on the gambler's two paths to perdition, winning and losing: "Both alike are lives of utter misery of spirit." But its "very long and very eminent usage" could not excuse *both alike*, said White 1870: "The phrase is not an idiom, and it is at variance with reason."

There are fashions in pique, however, and *both alike* is no longer a favorite target. Today's redundancy hunters have fresh outrages to denounce, like "free gift," "PIN number," and "hot water heater."

Brainy. Pure slang, and singularly disagreeable.

• • •

Brainy, said the English usagist H. W. Fowler, "is, and may as well remain, an Americanism." (He was wrong about its origin; the earliest *brainy* appears in an 1845 letter by the English poet Leigh Hunt.) Emily Post didn't think Americans should use the word either—at least not in "good society." But *brainy* had taken root in the American language, and why not? "It is hard to see why it is any more improper a coinage than *handy*," observed the Evanses in 1957, as they launched a counterattack. "Perhaps the British dislike of *brainy* is, at bottom, a dislike of brains," they said, quoting George Orwell on his Blimpish countrymen: "If you were a patriot you read *Blackwood's Magazine* and publicly thanked God you were 'not brainy.'" See *Smart*.

Bug for **Beetle**, or for anything. Do not use it.

• • •

Bug was already widespread in slang use to mean both "enthusiast" (gold bug, tariff bug) and "problem." Even the *Pall Mall Gazette* had printed it, though in quotes, in 1889: "Mr. Edison . . . had been up the two previous nights discovering 'a bug' in his phonograph."

But for the fastidious Bierce, *bug* probably had other drawbacks. Its use as a synonym for "insect" was considered an Americanism, hence inferior. And in England, where *bug* usually meant bedbug, it was an impolite word. In *The American Language* (1921), H. L. Mencken told of an American who, playing billiards with his English host, announced that he had killed a bug with his cue. To the Englishman, for whom all "bugs" were bedbugs, "this seemed a slanderous reflection upon the cleanliness of his house," said Mencken. Our "buggy" computers and "bugged" embassies would have bugged Bierce mightily.

Build for **Make**. "Build a fire." "Build a canal." Even "build a tunnel" is not unknown, and probably if the wood-chuck is skilled in the American tongue he speaks of building a hole.

• • •

"Build a fire" is "a common phrase, originating, probably, in the backwoods, where large fires are made of logs," said Bartlett in his *Dictionary of Americanisms* (1877). Though the English poet Robert Southey had used "build a fire" in 1805, the expression—like other creative applications of *build*—was predominantly an American locution. By the 20th century, though, no one but Bierce was complaining about the illogic of "building" fires and canals. Was he just being stubborn, or did his animus have a more personal source? Bierce had been San Francisco's star writer till young Jack London came to town, and Bierce was both critical of London's work and hostile toward his socialist politics. The two would meet, in 1910, at the Bohemian Grove and submerge their differences in drink. But in 1909, London was just an upstart rival—and the year before, he had published his famous short story "To Build a Fire."

Business for **Right**. "He has no business to go there."

• • •

"Mr. Thorpe had no business to invent any such message," says Catherine in Jane Austen's *Northanger Abbey*—and when Austen wrote, that sense of *business* was already a century old. The 20th-century attack on it, kicked off by Bierce, lasted only a couple of decades. "That usage writers from the first third of the 20th century should find something amiss about this use can be explained only by their ignorance of its history," says *MWDEU*. But Bierce's prejudice toward all commercial language might have been a stronger motive than ignorance.

But. By many writers this word (in the sense of except) is regarded as a preposition, to be followed by the objective case: "All went but him." It is not a preposition and may take either the nominative or objective case, to agree with the subject or the object of the verb. All went but he. The natives killed all but him.

• • •

In fact, since Old English, *but* has been used as both preposition ("everyone but him is going") and conjunction ("everyone but he is going"). Usage authorities have been wrangling over which is better since the 1830s, so there's no reason to heed anyone's counsel but your own.

But what. "I did not know but what he was an enemy." Omit what. If condemnation of this dreadful locution seem needless bear the matter in mind in your reading and you will soon be of a different opinion.

• • •

But what, like the older *but that*, is often called dialectal or colloquial, despite its use by some literary lights. Bierce ignores *but that*, leaving us to assume that the phrasing he prefers is "I did not know but he was the enemy"—standard English, but not, for many people, natural spoken English.

By for Of. "A man by the name of Brown." Say, of the name. Better than either form is: a man named Brown.

• • •

Remember the White Knight in *Through the Looking-Glass*, who explains to Alice that his song *is* "Ways and Means," but his song's *name* is "The Aged Aged Man," and the song's name is *called* "Haddock's Eyes"? Bierce's fellow usagist Alfred Ayres must have been a Lewis Carroll fan. In *The Verbalist* (1886), he tried to explain that "by the name" and "of the name" meant entirely different things: "One might know a man of the name of Brown, but know him by the name of Smith," he wrote. "That is, the man's name might be really Brown though supposed to be Smith. We say, then, 'I know a man of the name of Brown,' when we mean that we know a man whose name is Brown."

Actually, both "of the name" and "by the name" were common during the 19th century, and there's no reason to suppose that anyone—except possibly Alfred Ayres—was confused.

C

Calculated for **Likely.** "The bad weather is calculated to pro-duce sickness." Calculated implies calculation, design.

• • •

If Bierce had said that *calculate*, the plain verb, implies design, he would have been right. But *calculated*, the past participle, had taken a separate path. As early as 1722, the *OED* shows it being used to mean simply "suited, apt, likely to," in Daniel Defoe's *Colonel Jack* (1722): "The state of life that I was now in was . . . perfectly calcu-lated to make a man completely happy."

Some of Bierce's fellow critics also condemned the use of *cal-culated* for "likely, apt"—Richard Grant White was particularly hard on it—but Seth T. Hurd, in *A Grammatical Corrector* (1847), observed that the word was "used by respectable writers, in the sense of suited, fitted, adapted." The respectable writer he quoted was the 17th-century archbishop of Canterbury John Tillotson: "Religion is calculated for our benefit."

Can for **May.** "Can I go fishing?" "He can call on me if he wishes to."

• • •

Maybe Bierce really believed that the verb in his examples should always be *may*, but that wasn't the practice when Samuel Johnson invented the distinction between *can* and *may*, and it isn't today. The people who claim that *can* relates to ability and *may* to permission overlook the fact that *can* is also about "the realm of possibility dealing with what ought to be," explains *MWDEU*. This sense of *can* is ubiquitous in usage advice: "An unaccused offender cannot admit his guilt," says Bierce, but he doesn't mean that the offender is unable to admit it (*cannot*), or not permitted to (*may not*); he means the offender *should not* (because the right verb is *confess*).

As for the oral use of the verbs, whether you say *can* or *may* in asking (or granting) permission is more an etiquette question than a usage problem; it depends on who you are and whom you're addressing. But it's still not simple. As Bryan Garner notes in *Garner's Modern American Usage*, most educated people say *can't I* and *you can't* rather than *may I* and *you may not*, which sound stilted. In fact, "a fussy insistence on using *may* can give the writing a prissy tone." (Or the spoken words, I would add, since *can* vs. *may* comes up far more often in oral usage.)

Candidate for Aspirant. In American politics, one is not a candidate for an office until formally named (nominated) for it by a convention, or otherwise, as provided by law or custom. So when a man who is moving Heaven and Earth to procure the nomination protests that he is "not a candidate" he tells the truth in order to deceive.

· · ·

Bierce's analysis of *candidate* tries to shrink a general word to fit a specific American electoral situation. There is no linguistic or historical justification for limiting the word to nominees, however; the word *candidate* meaning "aspirant" dates from 1613, and has been applied to all sorts of candidacies—political, academic, and religious, electoral or not. You still occasionally hear people echoing Bierce, saying that the rafts of presidential hopefuls in primary season are not yet candidates for the presidency, but only for the nomination. Literally true, maybe; useful, no.

Cannot for **Can.** "I cannot but go." Say, I can but go.

· · ·

Robert Palfrey Utter, in *Every-Day Words and Their Uses* (1916), explained why Bierce (and others) disliked *cannot but*: "We are told that such an expression as 'I cannot but think,' meaning, 'I must think,' is illogical; 'I can but think' means 'I must think,' therefore 'I cannot but think' must mean the opposite." Logic, shmogic, said Utter: "If the phrase is illogical it certainly is idiomatic." Both *cannot but* and *can but* are still acceptable, though the first is more common. But these days we usually opt for "I can't help but go" or "I can't help going," bypassing the Biercean issue entirely.

Capable. "Men are capable of being flattered." Say, susceptible to flattery. "Capable of being refuted." Vulnerable to refutation. Unlike capacity, capability is not passive, but active. We are capable of doing, not of having something done to us.

· · ·

Since *capable* is derived from the Latin *capere*, "to take," Bierce thinks it should appear only with active verbs: "He's capable of going where angels fear to tread." But the passive construction was three hundred years old at the time—almost as antique as the active sense—and even usage commentators embraced it. Crabb 1818, for instance, wrote of "persons capable of being impressed"; Utter 1916 defined "practicable" as "capable of being put into practice."

Capacity for **Ability.** "A great capacity for work." Capacity is receptive; ability, potential. A sponge has capacity for water; the hand, ability to squeeze it out.

· · ·

"The distinctions between these two words are not always observed by those who use them," said Ayres 1881. He, like Bierce, thought *capacity* should connect with its root sense of "taking, having room for." The nuance has not disappeared: The current *American Heritage Dictionary*, in a note on synonyms, stresses *capacity*'s sense of "potential for acquiring" power. But Bierce's fondness for rigid boundaries tempts him to ignore the historical facts: *Capacity* has also meant "ability to perform or produce" at least since the 17th century. The *OED* quotes Jeremy Taylor ("the capacities of our Saviour and Lord," 1647) and Samuel Butler ("We are endued with Capacities of action, of happiness and misery," 1736) as examples of the "ability" sense.

Casket for **Coffin**. A needless euphemism affected by undertakers.

. . .

Casket, which meant a small decorative chest or box, had been borrowed as a word for a coffin only in Bierce's lifetime. An early example of the usage, in an 1844 directory for a Massachusetts trade show, listed "Two Black Walnut Coffins and one Mahogany Casket or Coffin" in one supplier's display.

Naturally, *casket* met with the sneers that euphemisms often provoke. Hawthorne, in 1863, called *casket* "a vile modern phrase, which compels a person . . . to shrink . . . from the idea of being buried." (Did he really think it was the word that caused that shrinking feeling?) Other critics called *casket* pretentious. Perhaps, suggested Edward S. Gould in *Good English* (1867), the obituary writer who uses the word is "intimating that a man in a 'casket' is not quite so dead as a man in a coffin." But as euphemisms tend to do, *casket* is becoming just another word for *coffin*; one day it too may sound rude and blunt, and another, sweeter euphemism will take its place.

Casualties for **Losses in Battle**. The essence of casualty is accident, absence of design. Death and wounds in battle are produced otherwise, are expectable and expected, and, by the enemy, intentional.

. . .

Casualties does, as Bierce suggests, imply chance events, but he was alone in his strangely abstract interpretation of the word. Ayres 1896, for instance, distinguished between *accidents*, which "are frequently occasioned by carelessness," and *casualties*, which "are altogether independent of ourselves." Bierce, however, says that a true casualty must be independent not just of "our" intentions, but of anyone's; the word should only be used of events that involve no motive at all. This narrow definition seems perplexing, even perverse, from a man who had been in combat. Of course warring enemies are trying to kill each other; but which individuals will end up killed or wounded is very much a matter of chance, as most people use the word.

Chance for **Opportunity**. "He had a good chance to succeed."

. . .

The other current sense of the noun *chance*—the one Bierce (we can assume) prefers—was "fortune, accident, luck (good or bad)." But his disapproval of *chance* meaning "opportunity" is hard to fathom; the usage had been known since 1300 or so, and was listed as standard in 19th-century dictionaries. Not surprisingly, Bierce used *chance* this way himself: In his short story "The Suitable Surroundings," an author says to an editor, "I have a right to expect that if you read me at all you will give me a chance."

Chin Whiskers. The whisker grows on the cheek, not the chin.

. . .

The America of Bierce's adulthood was a forest of facial hair, and Bierce—who is usually portrayed in a handsome mustache—had firm opinions on the appropriate terminology for it.

A few decades earlier, the word *mustache* had displaced *whiskers* for the upper-lip growth, and whiskers had moved to the cheek. Some people, perhaps trying to keep it all straight, started calling the beard *chin whiskers*. In an article in the November 1878 *Atlantic*, Richard Grant White reported that *chin whiskers* was "in very common use among all the Western people, beginning at the western part of New York." But like Bierce, he thought whiskers belonged on the cheeks: "The term 'chin-whisker' is not to be defended, and is both a solecism and, if I may be pardoned for saying so, a barberism." See *Goatee, Sideburns, Whiskers*.

Chivalrous. The word is popularly used in the Southern States only, and commonly has reference to men's manner toward women. Archaic, stilted and fantastic.

· · ·

Chivalrous, once a term signifying the valorous, chaste, and honorable conduct of the ideal knight, had shrunk by Bierce's time to the feeble sense we know today: "gallant toward the fair sex." None of Bierce's fellow critics bothered to mention the word; but then, they weren't former Union officers in the Civil War and saber-toothed satirists to boot.

Citizen for **Civilian.** A soldier may be a citizen, but is not a civilian.

· · ·

Bierce states it oddly, but he is probably objecting to the phrase "an ordinary citizen," once the equivalent of *civilian* in its looser sense. The "ordinary citizen," according to *The Columbia Guide to Standard American English*, was "one with only the powers and status conferred by that citizenship"—that is, someone who wasn't a soldier, policeman, judge, or other government official. Bierce may have found this use of *citizen* inaccurate and insulting, since it implies that soldiers are not citizens.

Claim for **Affirm**. "I claim that he is elected." To claim is to assert ownership.

. . .

According to Bierce, you can claim a thing—a right, an inheritance—but you can't claim *that* something is true; you can only affirm, assert, and so on. In fact, the "affirm" sense of *claim* had been quietly spreading for nearly two hundred years. But in 1870, William Cullen Bryant added *claim* to his list of words banned at the *New York Evening Post*, kicking off a controversy that lasted more than a century. *Claim* was here to stay, of course. In fact, as *MWDEU* notes, it can be a better choice than *affirm*, since it "introduces an element of doubt"—often a useful addition to a quotation in a news story.

Clever for **Obliging**. In this sense the word was once in general use in the United States, but is now seldom heard and life here is less insupportable.

. . .

Clever for "obliging, amiable" was an Americanism, current since the mid-18th century. (In New England, *clever* was also used of animals, meaning not "ingenious" but "good-tempered," a fact that *The Elements of Style* still finds worthy of mention.) As Bierce admits, this *clever* was already nearly obsolete; he was just giving it a kick to help it on its way.

Climb down. In climbing one ascends.

. . .

Bierce is following the lead of Frank Vizetelly, who, in *A Desk-Book of Errors* (1906), called *climb down* a needless American colloquialism. (He was willing to tolerate "crawl down" instead if the descent was "laborious, as though by hands and feet.") Robert Palfrey Utter tried to set them straight: "*Climb down* has been in use since 1300," he pointed out in *Every-Day Words and Their Uses*

(1916). Indeed, the *OED* finds the phrase in *Cursor Mundi*, a long religious poem composed before 1300: "Freely [we] may climb up and down" (spelling modernized). Utter's good sense did not prevail, however, for many decades; *climb down* was criticized at least into the 1980s.

Coat for Coating. "A coat of paint, or varnish." If we coat something we produce a coating, not a coat.

. . .

Bierce's ruling is pure invention, apparently; according to the *OED*, *coat* in the sense of "a layer of any substance, such as paint, tar, plaster, etc.," dates back to 1663. Jonathan Swift, himself a famous language nitpicker, wrote in *Gulliver's Travels*, "Over all is a coat of rich mould." *Coating* was the straggler; it didn't show up in the language till 1770.

Collateral Descendant. There can be none: a "collateral descendant" is not a descendant.

. . .

This is quibbling, or plain misunderstanding. Bierce seems to think *collateral* is a simple modifier of *descendant*, and that it's contradictory: If you're a collateral relative you can't also be a descendant. But *collateral descendants* are not descendants of each other; they're side-by-side offshoots of a common ancestor. As Webster 1913 says, "the children of brothers are collateral relations, having different fathers, but a common grandfather." This has been standard legal terminology since the 14th century.

Colonel, Judge, Governor, etc., for **Mister.** Give a man a title only if it belongs to him, and only while it belongs to him.

. . .

There's no Colonel Sanders or President Clinton in Bierce's usage book! And yet, says biographer Roy Morris Jr., after Bierce moved to Washington in 1901, he began using his Civil War military title "and was even listed as Major Bierce in the Washington telephone directory." (An earlier biographer noted that in Washington, "a man without a title is a social pariah"; another reported that Bierce protested the directory listing. Still, Bierce was clearly bending the rule he would endorse in print a few years later.)

Combine for **Combination**. The word, in this sense, has something of the meaning of conspiracy, but there is no justification for it as a noun, in any sense.

· · ·

Combine was already in use as a noun, short for "combined harvester," but that wasn't the word Bierce minded. He was objecting to *combine* meaning a private association for gain, especially for fraudulent gain; the sense was American, an upstart, an interloper. It didn't need Bierce's blessing, though. As Utter 1916 suggested, the word "was probably devised by writers of newspaper headlines to fit their spaces." And during *combine*'s short lifespan, that was justification enough.

Commence for **Begin**. This is not actually incorrect, but—well, it is a matter of taste.

· · ·

It was a matter of taste, and 19th-century taste, in both Britain and America, disparaged *commence* as a genteelism. "We never begin anything in the newspapers now, but always commence," grumped Henry Alford in *The Queen's English* (1864). "Careful speakers make small use of *commence* in any sense; they prefer to use its Saxon equivalent, *begin*," said Alfred Ayres in *The Verbalist* (1881). But though it may have been abused and overused, *commence* remains a respectable, if somewhat formal, synonym.

Commencement for **Termination**. A contribution to our noble tongue by its scholastic conservators, "commencement day" being their name for the last day of the collegiate year. It is ingeniously defended on the ground that on that day those on whom degrees are bestowed commence to hold them. Lovely!

· · ·

Did Bierce perhaps allow his disdain for the verb *commence* to color his feelings about *commencement*? Surely, after several years in England, he knew that *commencement* was Cambridge University's name for its graduation ceremony, even if he didn't know that the usage dated to the 14th century. Even in America, commencements had been going on for two hundred years—long enough that most people had managed to adapt to the usage, illogical or not.

Commit Suicide. Instead of "He committed suicide," say, He killed himself, or, He took his life. For married we do not say "committed matrimony." Unfortunately most of us do say, "got married," which is almost as bad. For lack of a suitable verb we just sometimes say committed this or that, as in the instance of bigamy, for the verb to bigam is a blessing that is still in store for us.

· · ·

Commit suicide does seem a bit institutional for such a drastic act, and "get" married a bit casual for such a ceremonious one. But euphemisms are no easier to legislate than other idioms; even Bierce used *commit suicide* more than once in his writing career. See *Suicide*.

Compare with for **Compare to**. "He had the immodesty to compare himself with Shakespeare." Nothing necessarily immodest in that. Comparison with may be for observing a difference; comparison to affirms a similarity.

· · ·

Syndicated language columnist James J. Kilpatrick, who could pick a nit with the best of them, confessed that he didn't get this one: "I will never in my life comprehend the distinction between compared to and compared with."

Many of his readers probably shared his bafflement. The *compare with–compare to* distinction—first proposed in 1847—is repeated in most usage books even today: *Compare to* means "liken," they say, and *compare with* means "contrast with." But following the rule is not so simple. People do tend to use *compare to* in the prescribed way, to mean "liken," says *MWDEU*: "I can only compare it to the color of the night sky" (Robert Penn Warren). But it's not always obvious whether a writer is trying to "observe a difference" or "affirm a similarity"; in many cases, you could read *compare* either way. And if you look closely at individual cases, you find significant minorities (on both sides of the question) using the "wrong" preposition. Does anyone really notice? Or are we all Kilpatricks now?

Complected. Anticipatory past participle of the verb "to complect." Let us wait for that.*

·   ·   ·

A century after Bierce wrote, *complected*—substituted for *complexioned* in expressions like "olive-complexioned"—is just about where it was: widely used and widely disparaged. The word, which debuted in 1806 in the journals of Lewis and Clark, "has a long history in American folk speech," says *AHD4*. In an earlier edition of the dictionary, *complected* was granted a status upgrade: "*Complected* has long been treated as a dialectal term in dictionaries, but it actually should be regarded as informal Standard English, since its wide distribution (including New England, the Midwest, the South, and elsewhere) disqualifies it as a true

---

* There is an English verb *complect*, "to interweave," based on the Latin *complectere*, "to plait," listed in *AHD4*, but it is rarely seen and not related to *complected* meaning "complexioned."

regionalism." *Merriam-Webster's 11th Collegiate Dictionary* adds that *complexioned* is losing the usage race, even in print: "Literary use, both old and new, slightly favors *complected*."

Conclude for Decide. "I concluded to go to town." Having concluded a course of reasoning (implied) I decided to go to town. A decision is supposed to be made at the conclusion of a course of reasoning, but is not the conclusion itself. Conversely, the conclusion of a syllogism is not a decision, but an inference.

· · ·

As *MWDEU* points out, the "decide" sense of *conclude* "goes back to the 15th century with Lydgate and Caxton." And Shakespeare too: "They did conclude to bear dead Lucrece thence." The usage was common in print at the turn of the 20th century, but critics had begun to denounce it; the attacks continued into the 1950s, but both the usage and the argument have abated.

Connection. "In this connection I should like to say a word or two." In connection with this matter.

· · ·

Bierce does not mind "in connection with this"—a phrase later usage critics faulted as flabby—but only its condensed form, "in this connection." He may have thought it was an Americanism—Bartlett 1877 called it "a New England phrase, used to such a degree that it has become quite shocking to nervous people." Wrong, said Tucker 1895: "in this connection" was used in Britain "certainly as long ago as 1780." But Bierce might have disapproved anyway; he registered a similar objection to "in our midst" as shorthand for "in the midst of us."

Conscious for Aware. "The King was conscious of the conspiracy." We are conscious of what we feel; aware of what we know.

· · ·

The king should be *aware* of the conspiracy, says Bierce, following a usage tradition dating from the 18th century—though if his courtiers are conspiring, he may also be *conscious* of a growing anxiety. Many writers do observe this distinction, consciously or not. But *awareness* and *consciousness* naturally have considerable overlap in the brain they have to share; mixing them up has never been considered a serious usage crime.

Consent for Assent. "He consented to that opinion." To consent is to agree to a proposal; to assent is to agree with a proposition.

. . .

There's no evidence that these words were ever much confused, but a number of usage writers have taken the trouble to explain the difference. "*Assent* respects the judgment; *consent* respects the will. We *assent* to what we think true; we *consent* to the wish of another by agreeing to it and allowing it," wrote George Crabb in *English Synonymes Explained* (1818). But Garner 2003 says the distinction is no longer an issue: "*Assent* is becoming less and less common; it survives mostly in formal uses."

Conservative for Moderate. "A conservative estimate"; "a conservative forecast"; "a conservative statement," and so on. These and many other abuses of the word are of recent growth in the newspapers and "halls of legislation." Having been found to have several meanings, conservative seems to be thought to mean everything.

. . .

Bierce was right in calling the "cautious" sense of *conservative* an innovation; it emerged in America only in the mid-19th century. But it had evolved naturally from *conservative* meaning "inclined to preserve," the sense in which the English Tories embraced the name in 1830. Within a couple of decades, American writers were associating the political brand of conservatism with the general notion of restraint: "He was rather too cautious and conservative" (1853); "Governor Cox was too moderate and Conservative to suit the Ohio Radicals" (1869); "We find girls naturally timid, prone to dependence, born conservatives" (1865). The usage hardly seems like reckless experimentation, unless, like Bierce, you're a language conservative.

Continually and **Continuously**. It seems that these words should have the same meaning, but in their use by good writers there is a difference. What is done continually is not done all the time, but continuous action is without interruption. A loquacious fellow, who nevertheless finds time to eat and sleep, is continually talking; but a great river flows continuously.

• • •

Bierce's division between *continually* and *continuously*, first enunciated by Elizabeth Jane Whately in 1851, remains the standard usage guidance. But the adverbs aren't so clearly distinguished in actual usage, notes *MWDEU*, and that's not surprising, since "*continually* had a 350-year head start on *continuously*." Writers often treat the words as equivalent, and since readers rarely object, apparently they do too.

Convoy for **Escort**. "A man-of-war acted as convoy to the flotilla." The flotilla is the convoy, the man-of-war the escort.

• • •

Bierce sounds very sure of his definition, but the dictionaries tell a different story. According to the *OED,* a *convoy* could mean a fleet or shipment of supplies under escort (the sense dates to 1577); or the armed forces doing the escorting (1596); or a fleet strong enough to defend itself (1605). Both the "escorter" and "escortee" senses appear in Webster 1828 and 1913. Since the verb *convoy* means "to escort, accompany," we might expect the etymologically alert Bierce to prefer the parallel sense—one that puts *convoy* in the active role of the escort—for the noun. But there's no accounting for his tastes.

Couple for **Two.** For two things to be a couple they must be of one general kind, and their number unimportant to the statement made of them. It would be weak to say, "He gave me only one, although he took a couple for himself." Couple expresses indifference to the exact number, as does several. That is true, even in the phrase, a married couple, for the number is carried in the adjective and needs no emphasis.

· · ·

Bierce's insistence that "a couple" isn't necessarily two—that inexactness is the point of "a couple" in this sense—was unusual; most language critics were busy denouncing *couple* as a sloppy synonym for any two things, related or not. And Vizetelly 1906, one of the few to mention indefinite *couple*, disagreed with Bierce: "Do not say 'He has a *couple* of dollars in the bank,'" he instructed. "Say rather, 'He has some money in the bank.'" Bierce, for once choosing usefulness over etymology, ended up on the winning side of this debate. *The American Heritage Guide to Contemporary Usage* (2005) interprets *couple* just as he did: "The sentence *She lives only a couple of miles away* implies not only that the distance is short but that its exact measure is unimportant."

Created for **First Performed**. Stage slang. "Burbage created the part of Hamlet." What was it that its author did to it?

· · ·

Created in this sense was borrowed from the French *créer un rôle*, says the *OED*. The usage appeared in the United States as early as 1855, in a review of a Boston performance of *Norma*: "Its popularity may be about one part in ten musical," the reviewer said of the opera. "The other nine parts are due to Pasta, who 'created the role' of Norma, and to Grisi, who with equal or more dramatic genius, reproduces it." This *created* is still essentially stage slang, but like so much specialized language, it is now widespread in journalistic usage.

Critically for **Seriously**. "He has long been critically ill." A patient is critically ill only at the crisis of his disease.

. . .

"Critically ill" still means "in a life-threatening condition, at a turning point"; the difference is that a century after Bierce wrote, medical expertise can make that critical period last longer than he could have imagined.

Criticise for **Condemn**, or **Disparage**. Criticism is not necessarily censorious; it may approve.

. . .

Criticism, the noun, does encompass approval as well as censure: "John Updike's criticism" does not refer only to his negative reviews. But Bierce was too late to retrieve *criticize*, the verb, for favorable notices. *Criticize* has been used (and heard) mainly as a negative since the beginning; that's why we coined the verb *to critique*.

Cunning for **Amusing**. Usually said of a child, or pet. This is pure Americanese, as is its synonym, "cute."

. . .

The *OED*'s earliest example of *cunning* dates to 1887: "As a child, she had been called 'cunning' in the popular American use of the word when applied to children; that is to say, piquantly interesting." The sense had evolved from an earlier American use of cunning to mean "quaintly interesting or pretty." Both seemed ridiculous to the language mavens, who knew *cunning* in its traditional sense, "knowing in a deceitful way, sly." But Vizetelly at least tried to be tolerant; in *A Desk-Book of Errors* (1906), he said *cunning* might be allowed to mean "bright, amusing," though it could not mean "dainty, choice." "A kitten may properly be said to be *cunning,* but not a brooch," he said. (And what about a brooch in the shape of a kitten? Vizetelly's editors were presumably male, and didn't think of that.)

Curious for Odd, or Singular. To be curious is to have an inquiring mind, or mood—curiosity.

· · ·

There are eighteen senses for *curious* in the *OED*; the one Bierce favors—*curious* meaning "inquisitive"—is the main "subjective" one (that is, describing the observer's mental state). For some reason, several of the 19th-century usage mavens decided this was the only legitimate sense. But *curious* in an "objective" sense, meaning "odd, queer, peculiar," is also completely respectable; its fully modern use dates only to 1715, but it evolved from senses like "artful, exquisite, choice" that stretch back to the 14th century. Webster 1913 quotes Shakespeare ("a curious tale") and Macaulay ("curious analogies") as illustrations of the usage.

Custom for Habit. Communities have customs; individuals, habits—commonly bad ones.

· · ·

The critics of Bierce's era agreed that we should distinguish between *custom*, a society's practice, and *habit*, a personal routine. "Custom respects things that are done by the majority, habit those which are done by individuals," said Smith 1893. But in practice, the words have never had sharp boundaries. The *OED* defines *custom* as "usage, fashion, habit (either of an individual or a community)"; one early example, circa 1340, refers to the "custom" among dogs of "berkyng & bitynge." Shakespeare and Jane Austen used *custom* instead of *habit* to mean one person's practice. And so did Bierce: "It had been my custom to throw the babes into the river which nature had thoughtfully provided for the purpose," he wrote in his creepy story "Oil of Dog."

D

Decease for Die.

. . .

Decease had been in use since the 15th century, but by the late 19th it must have begun to sound pretentious, euphemistic, or both; Vizetelly 1906, like Bierce, banned *decease* without explanation. The animus persists: Garner 2003 calls the verb "even more pompous than the noun."

Decidedly for Very, or Certainly. "It is decidedly cold."

. . .

Decidedly, said Webster 1913, means either "in a decided manner"—firmly, purposefully—or "indisputably; clearly; thoroughly." Why did Bierce think "decidedly cold" was improper? He may have believed the adverb needed a link to an agent, a "decider"; it would be in keeping with Biercean logic to say that a man might be "decidedly" angry, but a temperature could not be "decidedly" anything.

His fellow language critics, however, did not share his opinion. Decade after decade, we find them using *decidedly* to mean "very," in just the way he condemns: "decidedly modern" (Bache 1869), "decidedly un-English" (Hodgson 1881), "decidedly preferable"

(Vizetelly 1906), "decidedly vulgar" (Partridge 1954). The usage is decidedly correct.

Declared for Said. To a newspaper reporter no one seems ever to say anything; all "declare." Like "alleged" (which see) the word is tiresome exceedingly.

. . .

Bierce's is the first warning I know of against creative alternatives to *said*, but it wasn't the last. H. W. Fowler allowed *whispered*, *cried*, and even *groaned* as dialogue descriptions—those were verbs "naturally used after what is uttered"—but he drew the line at *she fluted*, *he doubted*, and *I scorned*. Theodore Bernstein, in *The Careful Writer* (1965), called the aversion to simple *say* "one mark of an unsure writer." William Zinsser (*On Writing*, 1985) urged: "Don't make your man assert, aver, and expostulate just to avoid repeating 'he said.'" And Elmore Leonard reduced their advice to its hard-boiled essence in *Elmore Leonard's 10 Rules of Writing* (2007): "Never use a verb other than 'said' to carry dialogue."

Defalcation for Default. A defalcation is a cutting off, a subtraction; a default is a failure in duty.

. . .

Until the mid-19th century, Bierce's definitions were right: *Defalcation* was a neutral term for "shortfall" or "curtailment," usually applied to revenues; *default* was the word that implied failure. But the terms were blurring, and in 1846, the *Worcester Dictionary* added a pejorative sense for *defalcate*: "a breach of trust by one who has charge or management of money." The usage traditionalists naturally resisted the change, but to no avail. *Defalcation's* transformation is now complete, says Garner 2003: "To be a defalcation, a deficiency in money matters must be fraudulent, and it must be by someone put in trust of the money."

Definitely for **Definitively.** "It was definitely decided." Definitely means precisely, with exactness; definitively means finally, conclusively.

• • •

Bierce's definitions are still valid, but a century later, Bryan Garner thinks the words "are increasingly confused." In *Garner's Modern American Usage* (2003), he sees *definitive* elbowing out *definite*: "He has some very *definitive* [read *definite*] views on golf-course architecture."

But this is not the first time the *definitely* alarm has been sounded. In 1889, in a "conversation" published in *Blackwood's Edinburgh Magazine*, one speaker says, "There is scarcely a paper I take up which does not inform us that something has been 'definitively arranged'—meaning, of course, 'definitely' or 'finally' settled." Perhaps the confusion between the words really has worsened over the past 110 years, but for now the verdict is "not proven."

Deliver. "He delivered an oration," or "delivered a lecture." Say, He made an oration, or gave a lecture.

• • •

Bierce must have imagined that *deliver* was pretentious, because the usage he dislikes wasn't new, nor was it wrong in anybody's book. Other language commentators used *deliver* in the way Bierce disapproved: "Time Ought to be allotted for the Foreigner to deliver twice over the Sentences he reads," said Robert Baker in *Remarks on the English Language* (1770). "If Mr. Everett were about to deliver his *oration* on Washington . . . would you say, "Let us go hear Everett *orate*?" asked Edward S. Gould in *Good English* (1867). The people in Bierce's supernatural tales saw things that weren't there; it looks as if he sometimes did too.

Demean for **Debase** or **Degrade.** "He demeaned himself by accepting charity." The word relates, not to meanness, but to demeanor, conduct, behavior. One may demean oneself with dignity and credit.

. . .

If you read Austen and the Brontës and Trollope, you already know *demean* in the sense Bierce prefers: "to behave, conduct oneself." But the other *demean* ("to lower, debase"), in circulation since about 1600, was gaining on it in the 19th century, with help from George Eliot, Dickens, Hawthorne, and other notable authors. Thackeray, in *The Four Georges* (1860), used the word in both senses: One prince "demeaned himself like a little man of valour," another "demeaned himself by marrying a French lady of birth quite inferior to his own." The newer *demean* was listed as standard in Webster 1913, and it is now the principal sense.

Demise for Death. Usually said of a person of note. Demise means the lapse, as by death, of some authority, distinction or privilege, which passes to another than the one that held it; as the demise of the Crown.

. . .

Demise began as a legal word, first for the transfer of an estate, then of a crown; starting in the mid-18th century, the word was also applied to the death that occasioned the property transfer. Bierce seems to think that *demise* is too elevated for daily use, and perhaps in his day it was pretentious journalese. Now, however, *demise* may be used lightly, or as a synonym for "passing" where *death* would be too literal. *MWDEU*'s examples include "his conveniently accidental demise" (*Life*, 1970) and "an Administration's demise" (*New York Times*, 1983).

Democracy for Democratic Party. One could as properly call the Christian Church "the Christianity."

. . .

Strange though it sounds, "the Democracy" had been the party's own nickname for itself since early in the 19th century. At the Democratic National Convention of 1852, several state delegations referred to themselves that way: "The Democracy of Pennsylvania hold principles higher than all other considerations." An 1898 article in the *Chautauquan* noted that when the Whig Party was dying, Ohio "went back to the Democracy again." Bierce didn't quite live to see the end of "the Democracy," but it would fade soon enough, upstaged in the 1920s by the opposition's new (and still nettlesome) nickname: the Democrat Party.

Dépôt for **Station**. "Railroad dépôt." A dépôt is a place of deposit; as, a dépôt of supply for an army.

· · ·

The casual use of *depot* for any train station was a very fat target for traditionalists. It was etymologically incorrect, as Bierce points out. It was also recent—dating from the first half of the 19th century—and it was American, hence by definition provincial. Most embarrassing of all was the native pronunciation, recorded in an 1842 account by Longfellow: "We were 'ticketed through to the depot' (pronouncing the last word so as to rhyme with teapot)."

No wonder the usage critics moaned. "Why we should ever have exchanged the sensible *station* of the English for the absurd *depot* of the French, is perfectly unaccountable," said Schele de Vere 1871. "Offensive to fastidious ears," said Ayres 1881. "Abominable," said White 1870. But the anguish had abated by the turn of the century, along with the usage. The June 1901 issue of *Correct English* told readers either word might be used, "although there is a growing tendency to prefer station."

Deprivation for **Privation**. "The mendicant showed the effects of deprivation." Deprivation refers to the act of depriving, taking away from; privation is the state of destitution, of not having.

. . .

As usual, Bierce would like the words to be discrete, but their senses had overlapped for well over a century; Webster 1913 gave *privation* ("want") as one synonym of *deprivation*. Today, both words have both senses, though the act of depriving is usually *deprivation*. "*Privation* is the more literary word," says Garner 2003; "its primary sense is 'the lack of life's ordinary amenities.'"

Dilapidated for **Ruined.** Said of a building, or other structure. But the word is from the Latin lapis, a stone, and cannot properly be used of any but a stone structure.

. . .

Dilapidate had been used since the 15th century to mean "fritter away funds," and to the philologist Richard Chenevix Trench, the word was a kind of "fossil poetry": "He who spake first of a 'dilapidated' fortune, what an image must have arisen up before his mind's eye of some falling house or palace, stone detaching itself from stone, till all had gradually sunk into desolation." That celebration of the metaphorical *dilapidate*, in an 1851 lecture, was itself poetic license; the root of Latin *dilapidare* meant "to scatter as if throwing stones," but even the Romans hadn't used the word literally. Bierce enjoyed the role of etymological fundamentalist, but he was virtually alone in suggesting that wood and brick buildings could not be "dilapidated."

Directly for **Immediately.** "I will come directly" means that I will come by the most direct route.

. . .

Directly had also meant "immediately" since Shakespeare's time, and that use was generally accepted. There were two newer senses of *directly* on the horizon that Bierce might have attacked, however. One was the American stretching of the meaning: While the British *directly* meant "immediately," the American version of the temporal sense meant "soon." The other was the use of *directly* as a conjunction (standard in Britain, but resisted in the United States): "Directly I saw the river I knew we were doomed." Here is something rare in the Biercean universe: a missed opportunity to cavil.

Dirt for **Earth, Soil,** or **Gravel. A most disagreeable Americanism, discredited by general (and Presidential) use. "Make the dirt fly." Dirt means filth.**

· · ·

"Make the dirt fly!" was Theodore Roosevelt's famous exhortation to the builders sent to dig (and blast) the Panama Canal into existence. And Roosevelt clearly had no aversion to *dirt*; he used the word several times in a 1906 letter to his son Kermit from the canal site. "The huge steam-shovels are hard at it," he wrote, "scooping huge masses of rock and gravel and dirt previously loosened by the drillers and dynamite blasters."

This idea that *dirt* wasn't always yucky was, as Bierce says, an Americanism. "A Southern lady will order her servant to 'fill a flower-pot with dirt,'" reported Maximilian Schele de Vere in *Americanisms* (1871), "and the foreigner is apt to be surprised at hearing people speak of *clean dirt*." Richard Grant White was not so dispassionate. "Dirt means filth, and primarily filth of the most offensive kind," he insisted in *Words and Their Uses* (1870). "A thing that is dirty is foul. The word has properly no other meaning." But his fellow Americans, surveying their swaths of unspoiled land, thought "clean dirt" was a fine and accurate description, and we still use the phrase, though perhaps less plausibly, today.

Distinctly for **Distinctively**. "The custom is distinctly Oriental." Distinctly is plainly; distinctively, in a way to distinguish one thing from others.

. . .

Yes, they are distinctly different adverbs. But the distinction probably didn't cause any more trouble a century ago than it does today.

Donate for **Give**. Good American, but not good English.

. . .

"Good American" should be good enough for an American, but earlier commentators had been even less charitable toward *donate* than Bierce. William Mathews thought the word was pompous: "Does it show a larger soul, a more magnificent liberality, to 'donate' than to give?" he asked in *Words; Their Use and Abuse* (1876). But *donate* found a defender in Frank Vizetelly, an editor of the *Standard Dictionary*, who quoted its definition in *A Desk-Book of Errors* (1906): "Donate should be used of the bestowal of important, ceremonious, or official gifts only." Deflate the language a bit, and that describes today's *donate*; we generally use the word of impersonal or charitable gifts, though we no longer insist that they be "important."

Doubtlessly. A doubly adverbial form, like "illy."

. . .

Doubtlessly and *doubtless* arrived hand in hand, around 1440, in an early Latin-English dictionary, and *doubtlessly* has appeared in dictionaries, unstigmatized, ever since dictionaries were compiled. Even so, it is not much used today. Occasionally a writer wants to make *doubtless* sound more adverbial, or feels the need for another syllable, and reaches for *doubtlessly*. But in edited prose, *doubtless* beats *doubtlessly* by roughly 12 to 1. See *Illy*.

Dress for **Gown.** Not so common as it was a few years ago. Dress means the entire costume.

. . .

Some of the Victorian usage gentlemen were indignant to see the general term *dress* being refashioned, over the decades, from a uni-sex word to a term for the garment they preferred to call a gown. "No man thinks of calling his coat or his waistcoat his dress," fumed Richard Grant White. "The origin of the perversion is prob-ably untraceable, except by the aid of some woman of close obser-vation and reflection, who is old enough to have been brought up to say *gown*. Such a person might be able to tell us how and why, in a little more than a generation, this word has come to be thus perverted by her sex only."

But there was no single cause; the terms *dress*, *gown*, and *frock* were just shifting in the breezes of fashion, both in Britain and in America. In 1901, the *OED* noted that *gown* was making a come-back "as applied to a dress with some pretension to elegance," and that *frock* had been relegated to the children's department. But an ordinary woman's dress would remain a *dress*, despite Bierce's hopeful prediction that the usage was a passing fancy.

E

Each Other for **One Another.** "The three looked at each other." That is, each looked at the other. But there were more than one other; so we should say they looked at one another, which means that each looked at another. Of two, say each other; of more than two, one another.

. . .

This rule was dreamed up in the 18th century, but never em-braced wholeheartedly by the usage fraternity—perhaps because it was so obvious that actual writers didn't obey it. Fowler 1926 scoffed that it was "neither of present utility nor based on historical usage." H. A. Treble and George Henry Vallins, in *ABC's of English* (1936), said, "The belief that 'each other' is restricted to two persons and 'one another' refers to more than two is harmless but unnecessary." Garner 2003 reluctantly agrees: "Careful writers will doubtless continue to observe the distinction, but no one else will notice."

Edify for Please, or Entertain. Edify means to build; it has, therefore, the sense of uplift, improvement—usually moral, or spiritual.

· · ·

Bierce's definition of *edify* was, and is, correct. But was anyone actually misusing the word? None of Bierce's contemporaries mention the issue. Garner 2003 says "edification" is sometimes misused for "enjoyment" or "titillation," but his examples look more like irony than error: "Hidden cameras record, for our edification, sundry couples' first kisses." And Bierce knew of this ironic sense; he used it himself, in his famous blast at Oscar Wilde, who toured the United States in 1882. Wilde, wrote Bierce in the *Wasp*, "has mounted his hind legs and blown crass vapidities through the bowel of his neck, to the capital edification of circumjacent fools and foolesses."

Electrocution. To one having even an elementary knowledge of Latin grammar this word is no less than disgusting, and the thing meant by it is felt to be altogether too good for the word's inventor.

· · ·

A blend of *electricity* and *execution*, *electrocution* was a novelty when Bierce wrote, and it might have met resistance on that score alone. But etymologists also hated the Latinate mashup that produced the neologism. "*Electrocute* is formed on the basis of *execute*, as if *cute* meant 'to kill,'" explained George Carpenter in *Rhetoric and English Composition* (1906). "But *cute* is merely a fragment of the Latin *secutus* (compare *persecute*), which means 'follow.'" Two decades later, *electrocution* was still shocking: Fowler 1926 called it a barbarism that "jars the unhappy latinist's nerves."

Today we've abandoned that battle, along with most of our Latin. The current usage debate is between those who insist that *electrocution* is fatal—as its coiners intended—and those who use it to mean a severe but survivable shock. The innovators say things like "fatally electrocuted," maddening traditionalists who call the phrase redundant. But several dictionaries have already decided that *electrocute* can mean "shock severely but not fatally." Bierce would be rolling over in his grave, if he had a grave.

Empty for Vacant. Say, an empty bottle; but, a vacant house.

• • •

An *empty* house, the commentators have advised for at least 150 years, contains no furniture; a *vacant* house might be stuffed with recliners and plasma TVs, but it would have no current occupant. George Frederick Graham, in *English Synonyms* (1857), waxed philosophical on the point: "A space is purposely left vacant which is intended to be filled up; a space is empty which is merely not filled up." Evans and Evans 1957 says that "though vacant is often used interchangeably with empty, it is usually applied to that which is temporarily unoccupied." It's clear that there's a distinction here; what isn't clear is that there was ever a usage problem.

Employé. Good French, but bad English. Say, employee.

• • •

The French and English versions of *employee* had been competing for more than half a century when Bierce wrote; Thoreau was among the early adopters of the Anglicized *employee*, having used it in *Walden* (1854). But it would be a few more decades before the native spelling could declare victory over the imported word.

Endorse for **Approve.** To endorse is to write upon the back of, or to sign the promissory note of another. It is a commercial word, having insufficient dignity for literary use. You may endorse a check, but you approve a policy, or statement.

• • •

The commercial taint of *endorse* came not just from its literal sense, but from its then-new use in retailing. "We have a promise of some advertising from a large brewer if we would editorially endorse their product," a Boston bicycling journal joked in 1897. But in both England and America, writers had been using *endorse* in the way Bierce found undignified for more than sixty years. "This book of Montaigne the world has endorsed, by translating it into all tongues," wrote Emerson in 1842. The verb was especially popular, for some reason, among theologians, who often endorsed, or declined to endorse, each other's views.

Usage authorities were not pleased. Henry Alford, author of *The Queen's English* (1864), could not bring himself to use the verb: "to endorse, I believe I ought to say, but I cannot," he wrote. In 1870, Bryant put *endorse* on his list of words not to be printed in the *New York Evening Post.* And Utter 1916 found a new fault in it: *Endorse* was self-important. "A man . . . who speaks of himself as endorsing an idea implies that without his support it might not pass current."

Fowler 1926 would endorse an argument—that far he would go—but not a product. But resistance was futile; in a century already well stocked with political candidates and soon to be awash in consumer goods, *endorse* would prove too useful a verb to snub.

Endways. A corruption of endwise.

• • •

In fact, *endways* is not a corruption but a synonym, just as old and respectable as *endwise*. Their origins are different, but both words date from the 17th century. Samuel Johnson may have led usagists astray, the *OED* suggests, when he wrongly declared in his *Dictionary* (1755) that *"way* and *ways,* are often used corruptly for *wise."* But not all usagists took his word for it. Several 20th-century commentators declared *endways* and *endwise* equally acceptable, and they remain so today. See *Lengthways*, *Sideways*.

Entitled for Authorized, Privileged. "The man is not entitled to draw rations." Say, entitled to rations. Entitled is not to be followed by an infinitive.

. . .

Where did Bierce get the idea that this use of *entitled* was faulty? The verb *entitle,* says the *OED*, is followed by "to with n[oun] or inf[initive]." Henry VII thought it was fine; a law enacted in 1495 speaks of "every man entitled to have the said penalty" (spelling modernized). The dictionary also cites examples from 1649 ("To intitle . . . the Queen to espouse") and 1741 ("every man thinks himself entitled to observe and to publish"). Bierce's objection— in which he is apparently alone—is silly.

But then, so is today's notion, current among some teachers and editors, that a book cannot be *entitled*, but only *titled*. Not so: This sense of *entitled* is the oldest, dating to the 14th century, when Chaucer wrote, "This booke . . . Entitled was right thus."

Episode for Occurrence, Event, etc. Properly, an episode is a narrative that is a subordinate part of another narrative. An occurrence considered by itself is not an episode.

. . .

"Properly," Bierce says, because *episode* in ancient Greek tragedy was the spoken part interpolated between two choruses. But the word had already broadened, a century before Bierce wrote, to mean "an incidental 'passage' in a person's life" or in a history, says the *OED*. And as almost every event is part of a larger narrative, it's hard to see where you would draw a line. Bierce called his famous short story "An Occurrence at Owl Creek Bridge"; but the characters in that tale might well protest that from their points of view, the *occurrence* was also an *episode*.

Equally as for Equally. "This is equally as good." Omit as. "He was of the same age, and equally as tall." Say, equally tall.

• • •

This little redundancy has provoked a lot of thunderous denunciation since the 19th-century prescriptivists noticed it. But it's easy to see why a speaker seeking emphasis might use the expression *equally as*, given its similarity to the perfectly respectable *just as* and *every bit as*. In this case, however, writers and editors have heeded the alarms about *equally as*. According to *MWDEU*, "its reputation is bad enough to make it relatively rare in edited prose."

Equivalent for Equal. "My salary is equivalent to yours."

• • •

Some usage writers went into numbing detail on this point: "*Equal* denotes that two things agree in anything that is capable of degree, as number, value, quality," wrote Albert N. Raub in *Helps in the Use of Good English* (1897). "*Equivalent* means equal in such proportions as affect ourselves, or the use we make of things." But as a journalist, Bierce was probably as attuned to the pretentiousness of *equivalent* as to its potential inaccuracy. He would surely have conceded that if your salary is paid in dollars and mine in cattle or whiskey, *equivalent* is the correct adjective.

Essential for Necessary. This solecism is common among the best writers of this country and England. "It is essential to go early"; "Irrigation is essential to cultivation of arid lands," and so forth. One thing is essential to another thing only if it is of the essence of it—an important and indispensable part of it, determining its nature; the soul of it.

. . .

Any solecism that is "common among the best writers" is no longer a solecism, but Bierce stuck to his antique guns. Perhaps he couldn't resist showing that he knew a stricter, philosophical sense of *essential*. But *essential* meaning "material, important" had been in reputable use for well over a century; as Bierce obliquely acknowledges, he had already lost this fight. See *Necessaries, Necessities*.

Even for Exact. "An even dozen."

. . .

The idiom "even dozen" is the relic of a use of *even*—to denote round, rather than fractional, numbers—that dates to the 17th century; Bierce is apparently the only critic who considers it a misuse. "Even dozen" may have survived because it contrasts with the still earlier "baker's dozen," or maybe just because we like the sound of it. As for the mild redundancy, peevologists need to learn that in language, that's a feature, not a bug.

Every for Entire, Full. "The president had every confidence in him."

. . .

"I had every confidence" is a usage problem, explained Vizetelly 1906, because "*every* is distributive, referring to a number of things that may be considered separately, while confidence is used as a mass-noun." The expression just squeaks by, he said, if you read it as elliptical for "every sort of confidence." The idiom had been in use for more than a century, however: "I have every confidence, that we shall find in the Americans a preference and a predilection in favour of their old connections," predicted a British parliamentarian in 1778. Garner 2003 calls the phrase "illogical, but an established casualism," but I'm not sure "casual" is correct; "every confidence," "every reason," and "every assurance" are used by diplomats and football coaches alike, and not always "casually."

Every for **Ever**. "Every now and then." This is nonsense: there can be no such thing as a now and then, nor, of course, a number of now and thens. Now and then is itself bad enough, reversing as it does the sequence of things, but it is idiomatic and there is no quarreling with it. But "every" is here a corruption of ever, meaning repeatedly, continually.

. . .

Bierce's dismissive description is correct: The phrase "every now and then" is nonsense, strictly speaking, and *every* is a corruption of *ever*. But Bierce was nearly alone at the barricades; other usage critics had accepted the phrase. As he said of "now and then," "it is idiomatic, and there is no quarreling with it."

Ex. "Ex-President," "an ex-convict," and the like. Say, former. In England one may say, Mr. Roosevelt, sometime President; though the usage is a trifle archaic.

. . .

Since *ex* was used in a related way in ancient Roman titles, and English from the 14th century on is littered with ex-consuls, ex-bishops, and ex-courtiers, it's impossible to guess why the prefix troubled Bierce. We do know that *ex* has bedeviled editors (and headline writers), for the reason Fowler 1926 noted: Prefixing a two-word title with *ex* can have puzzling results. Is the ex-Lord Mayor an ex-lord or ex-mayor? Maybe Bierce had tripped over the problem during his long career as a journalist, and banned *ex* for that reason.

Example for **Problem**. A heritage from the text-books. "An example in arithmetic." An equally bad word for the same thing is "sum": "Do the sum," for Solve the problem.

· · ·

Example seems to have been a math teachers' term for a couple of centuries; the *OED*'s citations run from 1674 to 1888. (*Sum*, labeled colloquial, comes a few decades later.) Whether Bierce objects to it as educational jargon or just wrong word usage is impossible to tell; apparently none of his fellow usagists shared his annoyance.

Excessively for **Exceedingly**. "The disease is excessively painful." "The weather is excessively cold." Anything that is painful at all is excessively so. Even a slight degree or small amount of what is disagreeable or injurious is excessive—that is to say, redundant, superfluous, not required.

· · ·

Bierce whittled this peeve to a fine point: When something is bad, he says, it can be *exceedingly* (very) bad, but to call it *excessively* (overly) bad implies that there's an acceptable amount of badness. But his fellow commenters went further, deploring even the positive use of the adverb, in expressions like "excessively kind," as nonsense.

In fact, Johnson's *Dictionary* had defined *excessively* as "exceedingly, eminently," citing Joseph Addison's use. But in the late 18th and the 19th centuries, *excessively* seems to have become a popular bit of hyperbole, as *awfully* and *frightfully* did later. Jane Austen used it copiously, often so as to gently mock the speaker: In *Sense and Sensibility*, the smarmy Robert Ferrars declares himself "excessively fond of a cottage."

And in an essay from the 1820s, a mother explains to her daughter that a scarf mustn't be described as "excessively pretty," because that means "too pretty." But Mamma, says the child, "every body says, excessively pretty, and excessively tall . . . What harm can it do?" Mamma answers that such "vague and exaggerated expressions" can lead to vague habits of thought and vaguer morals. But it wasn't till the 1880s that the usage posse took up Mamma's cause and united to stamp out *excessively*. They succeded, too—or maybe the fashion in hyperbole simply moved on.

Executed. "The condemned man was executed." He was hanged, or otherwise put to death; it is the sentence that is executed.

. . .

It is true that *execute* means "perform, carry out," as it has since 1477. But it has meant "put to death" for just as long: That sense appears in William Caxton's *Cato*, in 1483: "wherefor they be hanged or otherwise executed by justice." After four hundred years of unremarked use, this sense of *execute* was assailed by Latin-lover Richard Grant White, who insisted that it was, and always had been, nonsense. To execute, he said, is from Latin *sequor*, "to follow," and in English means "to perform; and how is it possible that a human being can be executed?" He urged writers to help eradicate this "vicious use," but Bierce was one of the very few to heed his call.

Executive for Secret. An executive session of a deliberative body is a session for executive business, as distinguished from legislative. It is commonly secret, but a secret session is not necessarily executive.

. . .

Bierce is uncharacteristically mild on this misuse of *executive*. Not so Gilbert M. Tucker, author of *Our Common Speech* (1895), who scoffed at "the ridiculous custom on the part of various voluntary associations and committees of resolving to 'go into executive session'"—as if they were U.S. senators—"when it is only meant that private business is to be taken up with closed doors. The blunder is doubtless largely due to the usual preference of ill-trained minds for fine and high-sounding words."

Expect for **Believe, or Suppose.** "I expect he will go." Say, I believe (suppose or think) he will go; or, I expect him to go.

• • •

The use of *expect* that was generally condemned in Bierce's time was "I expect you enjoyed it." "We cannot expect backward," said White 1870 (though people had been doing it for three centuries).

Bierce's "I expect he will go," however, had never been considered wrong. Perhaps he mistook the backward-expecting rule for a ban on *expect* with a *that* clause in every case. But his sentence is so innocent that in Evans and Evans 1957, its twin served as an example of correct usage: "I expect he will come."

Expectorate for **Spit.** The former word is frequently used, even in laws and ordinances, as a euphemism for the latter. It not only means something entirely different, but to one with a Latin ear is far more offensive.

• • •

Evans and Evans 1957 explains what Bierce is too squeamish to spell out: "To spit is, properly, to eject saliva from the mouth, but to expectorate is to bring up and expel phlegm from the lungs by coughing, hawking, or spitting." *Expectorate* was a 19th-century genteelism, and plain-spoken people as well as the Latin-eared found it distasteful. In 1903, a *New York Times* story headlined "USE OF THE WORD SPIT" reported that citizens were "objecting to the word 'spit' in the ordinances requiring that rules of common decency be observed." The head of the health department responded by pulling out a letter he'd received several years earlier from Theodore Roosevelt, then New York's police commissioner. "Can't you have our form of notice changed so as to read 'spit' instead of 'expectorate'?" Roosevelt had asked. "Expectorate is a vile word, and the Health Board ought to use good English."

Presumably the NO SPITTING signs stayed. The euphemistic *expectorate* did not; a user of the word "is now more likely to be trying for humor than politeness," says *MWDEU*, and even the humor has just about run its course.

Experience for **Suffer,** or **Undergo. "The sinner experienced a change of heart." This will do if said lightly or mockingly. It does not indicate a serious frame of mind in the speaker.**

• • •

Henry Alford would have called *experience* a specimen of psychobabble, had that word been current. The verb had infected the London newspapers, he complained in *The Queen's English* (1864): "No one *feels,* but *experiences a sensation*." He objected both to the verbing—"in the best English, *experience* is a substantive, *not a verb*"—and to the loose use of it; if we must employ the word, he said, it should retain its earlier sense of "experiment," or "have *personal knowledge of by trial*."

Several American critics followed his lead, but their campaign sputtered; after all, this sense of *experience* ("feel, suffer, undergo") had been spreading since the late 16th century. In 1917, J. Lesslie Hall defended *to experience*, saying Alford had not done his homework: "If the Dean had read the best English with this word in mind, he would not have spoken so dogmatically; he could easily have found it in Goldsmith, Gibbon, Lamb, Hallam, Poe, and other 'best English' writers," he said in *English Usage*. Alford was no longer around to experience the rebuke, but the verb continues to flourish.

Extend for **Proffer. "He extended an invitation." One does not always hold out an invitation in one's hand; it may be spoken or sent.**

• • •

Bierce sounds as if he's rejecting the figurative use of *extend*: Unless an invitation is hand-delivered, he suggests, it can't be extended. But English writers had been extending immaterial things for centuries; the King James Bible (1611) has "Let there be none to extend mercy unto him."

White 1870 had a different objection: He found the phrase pretentious. "The fondness for fine words leads lecture committees . . . to 'extend an invitation' to one distinguished man or other, instead of merely asking him, inviting him, or giving him an invitation." And Utter 1916 came up with still another: "Extend an invitation" was "condescending."

Clearly these critics weren't concerned with wordiness, so what was the problem they kept trying to give a name to? Probably "extend an invitation" was simply a vogue phrase at the time, hence irritating—as "perfect storm" and "it is what it is" are today—to the kind of people irritated by trendy language.

F

Fail. "He failed to note the hour." That implies that he tried to note it, but did not succeed. Failure carries always the sense of endeavor; when there has been no endeavor there is no failure. A falling stone cannot fail to strike you, for it does not try; but a marksman firing at you may fail to hit you; and I hope he always will.

• • •

Bierce is on to something here, but his formulation is too simple. *Fail* does imply an expectation somewhere in the equation, but not necessarily an attempt. You "fail" to show up at work, from your boss's point of view, whether you got stuck on the subway or simply went fishing. We say that a grenade failed to explode, but not that it tried to explode. (Even Bierce's falling stone could "fail" if it had seemed, even for a moment, likely to hit someone: "It dropped from a ledge just above him but failed to strike him.")

Fail has been used this way, to mean simply "not to do" or "to leave something undone" (especially something expected), since the 14th century. William F. Buckley Jr., well known as a language maven, demonstrated the usage repeatedly in a 1991 speech responding to a magazine article. "*Time* failed to note that under Reagan, 4.3 million Americans were relieved of any income taxation. *Time* failed to note that in the ten years before Reagan, we were all . . . paying progressively higher taxes . . . *Time* failed to note that the income cited in the statistics does not take into account the cash value of Medicare," and so on. Buckley's verb implied that *Time* should have noted those facts, not that it tried to but failed.

Favor for Resemble. "The child favors its father."

. . .

To favor, meaning "to look like" another person, was good English when Ben Jonson used it in a play in 1609 (as quoted in the *OED*): "This young lord Chamont Favours my mother." The verb arose from the 15th century use of *favor*, the noun, to mean "face, or countenance," as in Shakespeare's *Measure for Measure*: "A good favour you have, but that you have a hanging look."

Its fortunes had been sinking for some time, however; Lindley Murray, an American who lived (and wrote textbooks) in England, had decreed in his influential *English Grammar* (1809) that *resemble*, not *favor*, was the verb to use. By the end of the 19th century, "He favors his father" was considered colloquial in Britain and much of the United States, and colloquialisms were not Bierce's cup of tea.

Feel of for Feel. "The doctor felt of the patient's head." "Smell of" and "taste of" are incorrect too.

. . .

"The sauce tastes of cumin" is standard English, but "I tasted of the sauce" bothered usagists; Alfred Ayres, in *The Verbalist* (1881), called the *of* redundant. The construction was originally British, but Ayres (and probably Bierce) thought it was "a Yankeeism," and recommended using the plain transitive verbs *taste, smell,* and *feel*: "I tasted the sauce." The *feel of* construction lived on in some regions, though. The *Dictionary of American Regional English* notes that for some speakers the *of* marks a voluntary act: to *feel of* or *smell of* something is purposeful, in contrast to "feeling a chill," say, or "smelling smoke." The usage is now chiefly Southern, says *DARE*, and it's fading, if not as fast as Bierce might have wished.

Feminine for Female. "A feminine member of the club." Feminine refers, not to sex proper, but to gender, which may be defined as the sex of words. The same is true of masculine.

• • •

From Bierce's brief comment, you might conclude that he wants *feminine* and *masculine* to describe only grammatical gender, which would pretty much confine the terms to foreign-language classes. But he doesn't really mean that. He himself applies *feminine* to women; his taxonomy of refusals in *The Devil's Dictionary*, for instance, includes "the refusal absolute, the refusal conditional, the refusal tentative and the refusal feminine," otherwise known as—yuk, yuk—"the refusal assentive."

So what's his real point? My guess is that he just wanted to shoehorn "the sex of words" into this book; he liked the phrase, and the concept, enough that he treated it several times. He included *gender* (defined, again, as "the sex of words") in *The Devil's Dictionary*, and illustrated it with a bit of grammatical verse (note: *neuter* is a kind of intransitive verb):

> *A masculine wooed a feminine noun,*
> *But his courting didn't suit her,*

> *So he begged a verb his wishes to crown,*
> *But the verb replied, with a frigid frown,*
> *"What object have I? I'm neuter."*

And in a mini essay called "Lacking Factors," Bierce played with the idea that if words have gender, many are missing their mates. "Who ever heard of an alligatrix?" he asked. "The spinster—has she anywhere a femaler mate, the spinstress? I am told there is an article, a garment, if I have rightly understood—called a garter, and that it has commonly a mate, yet I know not if any one has seen a gartress." Where, Bierce wondered, are the hermit's *himmit*, the banshee's *banhee*, the hero's *shero*, the king of *Heba*? If he'd gone on for another paragraph, he might have ended up coining *herstory*.

Fetch for **Bring**. Fetching includes, not only bringing, but going to get—going for and returning with. You may bring what you did not go for.

. . .

Bierce is correct about the definition of *fetch*. But *fetch* and *bring* are rarely confused today, because most Americans now use *fetch* only in canine contexts. Bryan Garner suspects that may be why the word has "undergone depreciation," or gone to the dogs. In *Garner's Modern American Usage* (2003) he quotes Bergen Evans, who noted the fall of *fetch* some forty years ago: "Perhaps the command latent in it is resented as undemocratic. Or maybe its use in training dogs to retrieve has made some people feel that it is an undignified word." *Fetch* also "has associations of hick talk," adds Garner, perhaps because of its recurring role on *The Beverly Hillbillies*. Whatever the reason, *bring* vs. *fetch* is a forgotten issue; today the bone of contention is *bring* vs. *take*.

Finances for **Wealth**, or **Pecuniary Resources**.

. . .

Finances, plural, are "the pecuniary resources . . . *primarily*, of a sovereign state," says the *OED*, but the word can also be used "of a company or individual." Both uses were current in the 18th century: "My finances will never be able to satisfy these craving necessities," wrote William Cowper in 1766.

Webster 1828 had warned that *finances* was "most properly applicable to public revenue," but the 1913 edition of the dictionary merely noted that the word is "often used in the plural for funds; available money; resources." As a longtime journalist, Bierce must have seen this evolution in progress; surely he could have predicted that his fellow scribblers' hunger for lexical variety would trump their concern for terminological accuracy. See *Financial*, *Funds*.

Financial for **Pecuniary**. "His financial reward"; "he is financially responsible," and so forth.

. . .

The usage critics thought that *financial*, like *finances*, should stay in its institutional corral. "*Financial* is applied correctly to public funds or to the revenue of a government," said Vizetelly 1906, ignoring the facts of life and journalism. "*Monetary* and *pecuniary* apply only to transactions between individuals." Utter 1916 was more realistic. "In truth the distinction is seldom made, and seems hardly worth insisting on," he wrote. "*Financial* is now very generally used as the equivalent of any of the others."

Firstly. If this word could mean anything it would mean firstlike, whatever that might mean. The ordinal numbers should have no adverbial form: "firstly," "secondly," and the rest are words without meaning.

. . .

First, second, third is the preferred style of enumeration today, and Bierce was ahead of his time in recommending it. But dismissing the adverbial forms as "without meaning" is high-handed non-sense; *firstly* and its fellows date to the 16th century, and their meaning had always been perfectly clear.

When Bierce was a young reader, in fact, the style *first, secondly, thirdly* was common; Goold Brown (*The Grammar of English Grammars*, 1851) and William C. Fowler (*English Grammar*, 1855) recommended that sequence. *First* had so eclipsed *firstly* that when *firstly* began to reappear, it was treated as something new and unwelcome. Thomas de Quincey, in 1848, called it "a ridiculous and most pedantic neologism," and William Mathews, in *Words; Their Use and Abuse* (1876) put it on a list of "base coinages, barbarisms." H. W. Fowler defended *firstly*, however, in *Modern English Usage* (1926), and gradually the debate wound down. Life is calmer now that we've (almost) all agreed to use plain *first, second*, and *third*, but if you like a different style, you can probably find a usage expert who once endorsed it.

Fix. This is, in America, a word-of-all-work, most frequently meaning repair, or prepare. Do not so use it.

• • •

In *Americanisms* (1871), Schele de Vere called *fix* "the strongest evidence of that national indolence which avoids the trouble of careful thought." It's no surprise that Bierce, who shared the national anxiety about the propriety of America's language, would agree. But it is a surprise to find the usually sensible Bergen and Cornelia Evans, many decades later, channeling Schele de Vere. *Fix* is "a slatternly verb of all work," said the Evanses in *A Dictionary of Contemporary American Usage* (1957); it's "a sloven's word, avoiding even the faintest exertion towards precision."

This is just loony. As *MWDEU* points out, *fix* has fewer different senses than *take, set, do,* or *run,* and nobody calls these verbs slatternly. *Fix* for "repair" or "prepare" (a meal, a drink) dates to the 1760s; the *OED*'s first example is "A number of hands came to fix our whale-boats." The verb may never be elegant, but it is standard American, and it's spreading: These days even British newspapers occasionally refer to "fixing" a BMW or the world economy.

Forebears for **Ancestors.** The word is sometimes spelled forbears, a worse spelling than the other, but not much. If used at all it should be spelled forebeers, for it means those who have been before. A forebe-er is one who fore-was. Considered in any way, it is a senseless word.

· · ·

Bierce is correct about the origin of the word: *Forebear* started out as a combination of *fore* and *beer*, or "be-er," one who exists. *Forebear* (variously spelled) dates from about 1470, and nobody else seems to have registered any displeasure at its existence; it's a mystery why Bierce deems it unfit for wordhood.

Forecasted. For this abominable word we are indebted to the weather bureau—at least it was not sent upon us until that affliction was with us. Let us hope that it may some day be losted from the language.

· · ·

It's not the word *forecast* Bierce is abominating here, but the past tense *forecasted*, and that's fair enough: Since the past of *cast* is *cast*, it seems obvious that the past of *forecast* should be *forecast*. But verbs don't always follow their parents' rules, and *forecasted* has popped up here and there since the 16th century. Its numbers were sufficient to keep it in the reference books through the 20th century; both Evans and Evans 1957 (in America) and Partridge 1954 (in England) allowed either past tense, as did *The Columbia Guide to Standard American English* (1993). But Burchfield 1996 thought that Bierce's hope was being fulfilled: "After much rivalry between *forecast* and *forecasted*," he said, "the first of these has more or less ousted the other."

Former and **Latter**. Indicating the first and the second of things previously named, these words are unobjectionable if not too far removed from the names that they stand for. If they are they confuse, for the reader has to look back to the names. Use them sparingly.

. . .

Good advice then and now.

Fully for **Definitively**, or **Finally**. "After many preliminary examinations he was fully committed for trial." The adverb is meaningless: a defendant is never partly committed for trial. This is a solecism to which lawyers are addicted. And sometimes they have been heard to say "fullied."

. . .

Cassell's Dictionary of Slang (1998) suggests that *fully* may have been more beloved of "penny-a-line" journalists, eager to pad out their stories, than of lawyers. *Fullied* was pure slang, but in Britain—where *committed* means "put behind bars," either by "frivolous pretexts" or by due process—the phrase "fully committed" appears in some authentic legal writing. Joseph Chitty's *Practical Treatise on the Criminal Law* (1819), for instance: "When the party is . . . fully committed for trial, it is not usual to bring him from his first custody before a magistrate on a subsequent charge." Neither expression seems to have survived past the 1930s.

Funds for **Money**. "He was out of funds." Funds are not money in general, but sums of money or credit available for particular purposes.

. . .

Once again, as with *balance* and *financial*, Bierce tries to wall off commercial language from polite everyday vocabulary. But though *funds* usually has the sense he prefers, it has also been used loosely since the 18th century to mean "personal resources, available cash," according to the *OED*. "When he had no funds he went on tick," Thackeray wrote in *Pendennis* (1849). And "short of funds" became a common euphemism for a personal cash-flow problem: "At this I vaguely wondered, knowing that he was always short of funds," says the narrator of Henry James's "Maud-Evelyn" (1900).

Even in the 1950s, some usage writers still worried about money; Partridge 1954 and Evans and Evans 1957 cautioned that *funds* was an acceptable word for the amounts at one's disposal, but pretentious as a synonym for "cash" or "ready money." Maybe it was pretentious, or maybe it was just lighthearted; either way, it wasn't a usage problem much longer.

Funeral Obsequies. Tautological. Say, obsequies; the word is now used in none but a funereal sense.

• • •

Bierce's reasoning has the flaw common to other complaints about tautology: A phrase like *funeral obsequies* (or "nape of the neck," or "fatally electrocuted") is only redundant if listeners or readers know that obsequies must be funereal, napes are always on necks, and electrocution entails death. With unusual or shifting words, they often don't know; hence the helpful "redundancy."

Obsequies, however, had a more serious problem than obscurity. It was already associated with "important" burials, and by the mid-20th century it had come to sound pretentious; Partridge 1954 put *obsequies* (and its faithful companions, *mortician* and *funeral director*) on his list of "elegantisms." Today we solve both his problem and Bierce's by skipping *obsequies* entirely; if *funeral* won't do the job, *funeral rites* will.

Furnish for Provide, or Supply. "Taxation furnished the money." A pauper may furnish a house if some one will provide

the furniture, or the money to buy it. "His flight furnishes a presumption of guilt." It supplies it.

. . .

Bierce seems to think *furnish* should apply only to literal furniture.
But the verb had also meant "provide" or "supply with" for nearly
four hundred years, and most of Bierce's fellow usage writers employed it themselves in just the sense he deplored. Joseph Fitzgerald, in *Word and Phrase* (1901), did offer a mild caution,
observing that there was "a strong tendency in conversational use to
employ the verb Furnish to the exclusion of other terms." Why, he
asked, should one say, "'The hotel clerk furnished me with the key
to my room,' or 'furnished me with blotting paper'?" Surely some of
his readers would have had the obvious response: Why not?

G

Generally for **Usually.** "The winds are generally high." "A fool
is generally vain." This misuse of the word appears to come of
abbreviating: Generally speaking, the weather is bad. A fool, to
speak generally, is vain.

. . .

Generally had been used as a synonym for "usually" since about
1700. A few usagists of Bierce's generation tried to disentangle the
words, assigning *generally* to things done by many and *usually* to
things done often, but their campaign never got much traction.
And even Bierce was willing to "misuse" *generally* if it suited his
purposes: In *The Devil's Dictionary*, he defined it as "usually, ordinarily," so he could give a typically cynical example: "Men generally lie, A woman is generally treacherous, etc."

Gent for **Gentleman.** Vulgar exceedingly.

. . .

"Gent and Pants.—Let these words go together, like the things they signify. The one always wears the other," said Richard Grant White in *Words and Their Uses* (1870). Bierce's own definition of *gent* was "the vulgarian's idea of a gentleman. The male of the genus *Hoodlum*." *Gent* began as a jocular word, then spent close to a century being reviled as unspeakably vulgar, and now is jocular once more (or, in Britain, a word for the men's room). See *Pants*.

Genteel. This word, meaning polite, or well mannered, was once in better repute than it is now, and its noun, gentility, is still not infrequently found in the work of good writers. Genteel is most often used by those who write, as the Scotchman of the anecdote joked—wi' deeficulty.

· · ·

Genteel, like *gentleman*, had lost status when it was taken up by the wrong sort of people. Bierce also recorded its decline in *The Devil's Dictionary*; *genteel*, he said there, means "refined, after the fashion of a gent," and he elaborated in verse:

> *Observe with care, my son, the distinction I reveal:*
> *A gentleman is gentle and a gent genteel.*
> *Heed not the definitions your "Unabridged" presents,*
> *For dictionary makers are generally gents.*

As for "the Scotchman of the anecdote," he was Charles Maclaren, editor of the *Scotsman* until the 1840s, and the anecdote was one retold in several publications during the 1880s. The *Canadian Monthly*'s account calls Maclaren a "hardheaded, sagacious, unhumorous Scotsman" who "could in a manner see [a joke], but certainly he could not *feel* it." Then, as the story goes, Maclaren hired a jolly assistant, and "he could only marvel mutely . . . at the exuberance of humour and the fertility of resource of his sub-editor. In perfect astonishment he observed that his young man could joke on everything. 'Now,' added he, 'for my pairt I can joke, but then I joke with deeficulty.'"

Gentleman. It is not possible to teach the correct use of this overworked word: one must be bred to it. Everybody knows that it is not synonymous with man, but among the "genteel" and those ambitious to be thought "genteel" it is commonly so used in discourse too formal for the word "gent." To use the word gentleman correctly, be one.

· · ·

Maybe it was impossible to teach the use of *gentleman*, but other usage writers gave it a shot. "Well-bred men, men of culture and refinement—gentlemen, in short—use the terms *lady* and *gentleman* comparatively little, and they are especially careful not to call themselves gentlemen," wrote Alfred Ayres in *The Verbalist* (1881). Hand-wringing over the democratization—or debasement—of *gentleman* went on for decades, on both sides of the Atlantic. Even in 2003, *Garner's Modern American Usage* cautioned that the word "should not be used indiscriminately as a genteelism for *man*," but reserved for "a cultured, refined man." But gentlemen, for better or worse, aren't what they used to be, and neither is our level of interest in who deserves the name.

Genuine for **Authentic**, or **Veritable**. "A genuine document," "a genuine surprise," and the like.

· · ·

J. H. Long, in *Slips of Tongue and Pen* (1889), explained what Bierce is getting at: "*Authentic* is that which gives a true account of the matters in question. *Genuine* is that which has been written or composed by the person whose signature the book or paper bears." The distinction had been developed by 18th-century Bible scholars to describe their sources, but it was too slippery for most people to grasp, and even usage writers didn't show much interest. "Today the words are interchangeable in most sentences," says Garner 2003.

Given. "The soldier was given a rifle." What was given is the rifle, not the soldier. "The house was given a coat (coating) of paint." Nothing can be "given" anything.

· · ·

"The soldier was given a rifle" seems utterly ordinary to modern ears, and the construction had been common for centuries. But some critics decided the usage—a passive verb with a "retained object"—was illegitimate, because both nouns, they said, were treated as objects of the verb. "A rifle was given to the soldier" had a proper subject of its passive verb; but the soldier wasn't being "given," and could not be the subject.

Alfred Ayres, in *The Verbalist* (1881), pointed out that you could solve the problem by treating the first object as dative case—reading it as "(To) the soldier was given a rifle." Of course, that meant that when the sentence began with a pronoun, it would have to be "Him was given a rifle"—odd, perhaps, but at least grammatically correct, Ayres thought.

Bosh! replied Thomas Lounsbury, the American scholar and language critic. In *The Standard of Usage in English* (1908) he listed several pages of quotations using the "barbaric" retained object. (Samuel Johnson, for example: "In the library I was shown some curiosities.") "Here is an idiom which has been employed for more than six centuries. For the last three of these it has been in use by every writer whom we regard as an authority," wrote Lounsbury. It was preposterous, he said, to think of abandoning a useful and familiar construction "because it offends the linguistic sensibilities of some men who have studied grammar without studying the literature upon which any grammar entitled to consideration is based."

Goatee. In this country goatee is frequently used for a tuft of beard on the point of the chin—what is sometimes called "an imperial," apparently because the late Emperor Napoleon III wore his beard so. His Majesty the Goat is graciously pleased to wear his beneath the chin.

. . .

Goatee was an American coinage, and probably not much older than Bierce—the *OED*'s first citation dates from 1844—so he may well have considered it hayseedy, ill-formed slang. Or maybe, as a clean-chinned kind of guy, he just disliked the style. See *Chin Whiskers, Sideburns, Whiskers.*

Got Married for **Married.** If this is correct we should say, also, "got dead" for died; one expression is as good as the other.

. . .

Get married, in general use since the mid-17th century, was one of many expressions (*get acquainted, get killed, get distracted*) in which, as the *OED* says, *get* "[takes] the place of *be* as a passive-forming auxiliary." Bierce pretends to believe that if some past participles pair up with *get,* all past participles must be allowed to do so, but he knows that isn't the way language works.

Gotten for **Got.** This has gone out of good use, though in such compounded words as begotten and misbegotten it persists respectably.

. . .

Reports of *gotten*'s death, during much of the 19th century, were greatly exaggerated. It was indeed dwindling in British English, and Lindley Murray, writing in England, called it almost extinct in his popular *English Grammar* (1809). American usagists and teachers echoed his opinion, but in this country *gotten* survived; Americans today use both *got* and *gotten*, more or less interchangeably, as the past participle.

Graduated for Was Graduated.

· · ·

The verb *to graduate* was in transition a century ago; the older passive, "Joe was graduated from college," was being supplanted by "Joe graduated from college." ("To graduate college," without the preposition, was not yet on the horizon.) In *A Desk-Book of Errors* (1906), Frank Vizetelly noted that the use "has been condemned by purists but is now well established. Thus, one may correctly say 'He *was graduated* from a university' or '*He graduated* from a university.'" And J. Lesslie Hall, in *English Usage* (1917), reported that "he graduated from" was dominant in the text of *Encyclopaedia Britannica*, "which shows that the active form is used regularly in England."

This evidence did not persuade everyone; the Biercean orthodoxy was stoutly defended into the 1980s. And then, of course, along came "Joe graduated college" to scandalize traditionalists. The goalposts have moved, but the contest goes on.

Gratuitous for Unwarranted. "A gratuitous assertion." Gratuitous means without cost.

· · ·

Gratuitous did mean "without cost"—"he gave a gratuitous concert"—but it also meant "uncalled-for, unjustified, asserted without evidence," as it had for the past two centuries. Apparently these related senses were falling out of favor—White 1870 called them "affected"—and one of the specific applications has disappeared: We no longer call a flaky, unsupported theory a "gratuitous hypothesis." But the "uncalled-for," "unnecessary-roughness" meaning—"gratuitous insult," "gratuitous criticism," and the like—has not only survived but flourished.

Grueling. Used chiefly by newspaper reporters; as, "He was subjected to a grueling cross-examination." "It was grueling weather." Probably a corruption of grilling.

. . .

Grueling is not related to *grilling*, but it is also a food metaphor. It is rooted in *gruel*, the runny porridge, considered as a punishment. "To take one's gruel" dates from the late 18th century, says the *OED*, the verb (and participle) to the mid-19th. Bierce knows *grueling* is new, and suspects it of slanginess; naturally he doesn't like it.

Gubernatorial. Eschew it; it is not English, is needless and bombastic. Leave it to those who call a political office a "chair." "Gubernatorial chair" is good enough for them. So is hanging.

. . .

Yes, *gubernatorial* is a bit unwieldy, and yes, it seems to be based on the nonexistent Latin *gubernatorius*. (*Gubernator* was good Latin, but not a good foundation for an adjective, according to the purists.) White 1870 called it a "clumsy piece of verbal pomposity"; he thought *governor's* was adjective enough. Ralcy Husted Bell, in *The Worth of Words* (1902), said that only "pedants and 'small potatoes' use this word," though he stopped short of recommending the death penalty. But *gubernatorial* had been around for a century and a half before the wave of word rage hit; if there's a better way to say "pertaining to a governor," we still haven't managed to unearth it.

H

Had Better for **Would Better.** This is not defensible as an idiom, as those who always used it before their attention was directed to it take the trouble to point out. It comes of such contractions as *he'd* for *he would*, *I'd* for *I would*. These clipped words are erroneously restored as "he had," "I had." So we have such monstrosities as "He had better beware," "I had better go."

• • •

Bierce's explanation for the origin of *had better* has no historical validity; it was dreamed up by an 18th-century grammarian who decided that *had better*, *had rather*, and *had best* made no sense, and therefore must be errors. They are not. Thomas Lounsbury, in *The Standard of Usage in English* (1908), scolded earlier grammarians for "correcting" *had better* to *would better* simply because they couldn't explain how *had better* was parsed. But he admitted it wasn't easy: "The idiom . . . presents a very genuine difficulty which has perplexed generations of men." Lounsbury explained how *had better* had evolved from the 13th-century *had liefer*, and the fit of grammatical anxiety passed. *Had better* is good English again, though *would better* is now accepted as well.

Hail for **Come.** "He hails from Chicago." This is sea speech, and comes from the custom of hailing passing ships. It will not do for serious discourse.

• • •

All right then, Major Bierce, sir—we'll make sure not to say that you "hail from" San Francisco, or from Horse Cave Creek, Ohio. At least not where you can hear us.

Have Got for **Have.** "I have got a good horse" directs attention rather to the act of getting than to the state of having, and represents the capture as recently completed.

• • •

Bierce criticizes *have got* not (as some people now do) because it's a wordy version of *have*, but because he thinks it can only mean "have acquired." "I've got a new car," in his view, means not "I own a new car" but "I recently bought a car." Bierce believed that *got-ten* was disappearing from the language (as it was in Britain, though not in America), and that *got* must be replacing it. It was all an illusion; Americans kept on using *have got* for "have" ("I've got a secret") and *gotten* for "acquired or become" ("they've gotten divorced"). See *Got Married, Gotten*.

Head over Heels. A transposition of words hardly less surprising than (to the person most concerned) the mischance that it fails to describe. What is meant is heels over head.

· · ·

Heels over head it once was, starting in the 14th century, but during the 1700s the phrase somersaulted to *head over heels*. By the time Bierce protested, people had been complaining about the expression for at least half a century—"a very common but very low phrase," Seth T. Hurd called it in *A Grammatical Corrector* (1847). And a century after Bierce, a few diehards are still complaining about the upside-down idiom, as fruitlessly as ever.

Healthy for Wholesome. "A healthy climate." "A healthy occupation." Only a living thing can be healthy.

· · ·

The *OED*'s first citation for *healthy*, dated 1552, quotes an English-Latin dictionary that gives *healthful* and *healthy* as synonyms. Over the next three centuries, various writers referred to healthy places, healthy herbs, and healthy recreations. Then Alfred Ayres decided to improve the language. In *The Verbalist* (1881), he explained that foods could not be "healthy"; the proper language was "A *healthy* ox makes *wholesome* food." (Ayres reserved *healthful* for things like climate and exercise.)

Ayres and his followers spread the gospel of *healthful* to English teachers and newspaper editors throughout the nation, and copy editors enforce it even today. But in truth, "a healthy climate" has never been bad English. "If you observe the distinction . . . you are absolutely correct, and in the minority," says *MWDEU*. "If you ignore the distinction you are absolutely correct, and in the majority."

Helpmeet for **Helpmate**. In Genesis Adam's wife is called "an help meet for him," that is, fit for him. The ridiculous word appears to have had no other origin.

. . .

"Here we have a comedy of errors," said Theodore Bernstein in *Miss Thistlebottom's Hobgoblins* (1971). First came the King James Bible's "an help meet for him." In Error No. 1, said Bernstein, the words were hyphenated, then squashed into a single word, *helpmeet*. "Then came Error No. 2 when some writers apparently thought that *helpmeet* didn't make any sense—which it didn't—and decided the proper word must be *helpmate*. And so today we are stuck with two corrupted words."

Helpmate, however, at least looks plausible, and after three hundred years we're used to it. But Bierce must not have known of its fishy derivation; if he had, he would surely have mocked it, along with *helpmeet*, as an etymological monster.

Hereafter for **Henceforth**. Hereafter means at some time in the future; henceforth, always in the future. The penitent who promises to be good hereafter commits himself to the performance of a single good act, not to a course of good conduct.

. . .

"Can anything be more clear than the difference of meaning between these two words?" demanded Henry H. Breen in *Modern English Literature: Its Blemishes and Defects* (1857). "And yet, how often do we see them misapplied." How often *did* he see them misapplied, I wonder? Yes, *henceforth* means "from now on" and *hereafter* "in the future," and it's not hard to imagine *hereafter* being stretched to mean (correctly or not) "at all times in the future." But if there was rampant confusion, the other usage critics seem to have missed it.

Honeymoon. Moon here means month, so it is incorrect to say, "a week's honeymoon," or, "Their honeymoon lasted a year."

. . .

And while we're being literal-minded, what about that "honey"? If the newlyweds should fight, after all, it wouldn't be a sweet time.

According to Theodore Bernstein, newspapers have been known to ban *honeymoon* on grounds of inaccuracy (though I've always thought they preferred "wedding trip" because it sounded classier). But according to the *OED*, the original "honeymoon" metaphor, which dates from the 1500s, had nothing to do with duration; it was comparing the couple's love to the moon, "which is no sooner full than it begins to wane." Or as a 17th-century writer put it: "It is hony now, but it will change as the Moon." Bierce's etymology is correct, but irrelevant.

Horseflesh for Horses. A singularly senseless and disagreeable word which, when used, as it commonly is, with reference to hippophilism, savors rather more of the spit than of the spirit.

. . .

Horseflesh meant the living animals a century before it was used for "horsemeat," and "a good judge of horseflesh," even in Bierce's day, was not a chef but someone who could help you buy (or bet on) a horse. Bierce's heavy-handed joke is that *flesh* makes him think of barbecuing horses, not riding and racing and admiring them. He was the only usage commentator to register a complaint; did the horsemeat he tried in Paris leave a bad taste?

Humans as a Noun. We have no single word having the general yet limited meaning that this is sometimes used to express—a

meaning corresponding to that of the word animals, as the word men would if it included women and children. But there is time enough to use two words.

• • •

Nobody knows why the usage critics of the later 19th century decided that *human*, after four hundred years as an English noun, should henceforth be an adjective only. The earliest reference to the "rule" that I've found appeared in an 1871 essay in the *Southern Review*: "Some uneducated people . . . [say] not that a man is a human being, but that he is simply 'a human.'" The same year, Maximilian Schele de Vere defended *human* as a noun, noting, in *Americanisms*, that "Chapman uses it habitually in his translation of Homer, and his example is followed by a host of English writers."

But the anti-*human* fashion caught on, and for most of the 20th century—despite the resistance of well-known usage commentators—many teachers and editors insisted that "human beings" was the correct expression. The notion could be found in usage handbooks into the 1970s, and it probably lingers still in some professorial and editorial heads.

Hung for **Hanged**. A bell, or a curtain, is hung, but a man is hanged. Hung is the junior form of the participle, and is now used for everything but man. Perhaps it is our reverence for the custom of hanging men that sacredly preserves the elder form—as some, even, of the most zealous American spelling reformers still respect the u in Saviour.

• • •

Both the regular and the irregular *hang* date to the year 1000 or earlier; if *hung* is "the junior form" of the past tense (and participle), it's only because it was spelled *heng* and *hong* in its early years, not because it's a latecomer to the language. As for which word hangs the man and which the curtain, the distinction wasn't especially important to most 19th-century grammarians, says *MWDEU*;

dictionaries often treated the two forms as simple variants. It was only in the 20th century that the *hanged*-is-for-people convention became a firm schoolroom-and-newsroom rule. (*Hanged* may have hung on in that one role, says *MWDEU*, "because it was the form favored by judges in pronouncing sentence.") The distinction is still enforced at most publications, but *hung* is quite widely used as an informal variant of *hanged*.

Hurry for **Haste** and **Hasten**. To hurry is to hasten in a more or less disorderly manner. Hurry is misused, also, in another sense: "There is no hurry"—meaning, There is no reason for haste.

· · ·

The grammarians of Bierce's day made much of the distinction between *hasten*, which meant simply "go rapidly," and *hurry*, which they said implied some degree of fuss and hubbub. The distinction was real, though hardly rigid; the proverb is "Haste makes waste," after all, not "Hurry makes waste."

But the nitpickers' point was more about social differences than sense: *To hasten* could be dignified, *to hurry* never. "Richardson calls hurry a female word, and, perhaps, women do make use of it oftener than men," observed Hester Lynch Piozzi in *British Synonymy* (1804). "Men may hasten; children hurry," wrote George Crabb in *English Synonymes* (1818). And Oliver Wendell Holmes quoted the maxim "Nothing so vulgar as to be in a hurry" (1859). Now that our busyness is a badge of honor, a sign that we're in demand, a horror of hurrying seems antiquated indeed.

Hurt for **Harm**. "It does no hurt." To be hurt is to feel pain, but one may be harmed without knowing it. To spank a child, or flout a fool, hurts without harming.

· · ·

Hurt is the more general term; it has meant both "give pain to" and "injure" since the 13th century. *Harm* is more limited; as Bierce says, it means only "injure, damage," with or without pain. Bierce would like *hurt* to be restricted to the "pain" sense, and *harm* applied only to injuries. His urge to declutter the language is understandable (and habitual), but simply proclaiming that *hurt* can't mean *harm* doesn't make it so.

I

Idea for **Thought, Purpose, Expectation**, etc. "I had no idea that it was so cold." "When he went abroad it was with no idea of remaining."

• • •

Richard Chenevix Trench had lamented the fate of *idea* in *English Past and Present* (1855): "How infinite the fall of this word since the time when Milton sang of the Creator contemplating his newly created world . . . 'Answering his great *idea*,' to its present use when this person 'has an *idea*, that the train has started,' and the other 'had no *idea* that the dinner would be so bad.'" Trench quoted Johnson on the proper sense of *idea*: "something of which an image can be formed in the mind."

Bierce doesn't spell out his definition of *idea*, but he seems to have been less strict than Trench. In his writing, he used *idea* both for broad concepts—"the Malthusian idea," "the republican idea"— and as a synonym for "notion": In 1908 he wrote to his boss, William Randolph Hearst, "I despair of making you understand my letters, for you seem to have the fixed idea that they are ugly." That sounds awfully similar to the casual uses Trench deplored, but then, *idea* had never been as pure and simple as Trench pretended.

Identified with. "He is closely identified with the temperance movement." Say, connected.

. . .

Bierce would surely have despised the modern psychological use of *identify with*, as in "I identify with her because we both have twins." Maybe even the 19th-century usage sounded like psychobabble to him; but it was a natural outgrowth of "to identify oneself with," meaning "to associate inseparably," a sense Edmund Burke had used in 1780 (as quoted in the *OED*): "Let us identify, let us incorporate ourselves with the people."

Ilk for Kind. "Men of that ilk." This Scotch word has a narrowly limited and specific meaning. It relates to an ancestral estate having the same name as the person spoken of. Macdonald of that ilk means, Macdonald of Macdonald. The phrase quoted above is without meaning.

. . .

Bierce is right about the former meaning of *ilk*, and usage writers kept trying to set us straight into the 1960s. But in 1957, Evans and Evans ruled that *ilk* for "kind" had become "not only an acceptable meaning but the primary meaning" (*A Dictionary of Contemporary American Usage*). Garner 2003 agrees: "Because there is little call outside Scotland for the original sense, the extended sense must be accepted as standard." Perhaps Bierce would have softened toward *ilk* if he could have foreseen what the *OED*'s lexicographers would find when they came to the *I* volume: The oldest example of the "erroneous" *ilk* appears in the lines, "As if she was a lady, An' that indeed, o' nae sma' ilk"—lines from a 1790 poem by the Scotsman James Fisher.

Illy for Ill. There is no such word as illy, for ill itself is an adverb.

. . .

Alfred Ayres had declared *illy* nonexistent in *The Verbalist* (1881), but Samuel Fallows, in *Discriminate* (1885), disagreed. *Ill* may be better, he said, but "those writers are in error, who say there is no such word as *illy* in our language. Southey says, 'I have illy spared so large a band.' Its use, however, is rare."

Speakers have always been tempted to end their adverbs with *-ly*—see Bierce on *doubtlessly* and *offhandedly*—and *illy* had been around since the mid-16th century. According to *MWDEU*, the usage persisted long enough to spawn, in 1931, an Illy Haters Union—a group described in the *New York Sun* as "desperate and determined" in opposing the adverb. And it looks as if they succeeded; outside of crossword puzzles, hip-hop lyrics, and the coffee aisle of Whole Foods, *illy* is rarely seen now.

Imaginary Line. The adjective is needless. Geometrically, every line is imaginary; its graphic representation is a mark. True the text-books say, draw a line, but in a mathematical sense the line already exists; the drawing only makes its course visible.

•   •   •

Bierce may be the only usagist who tried to ban *imaginary line*, but he wasn't the only writer eager to show that he knew basic geometry. A book review in the *Literary World*, in 1851, observed that "we often, indeed, hear a cord or a rope called a line, but every one understands this to imply a loose use of language."

"Loose use of language"? No. *Line* already meant "rope" or "string" in the year 1000. The mathematical definition—"A lyne is a magnitude having one onely space or dimension" (*OED*)—didn't come along till the 16th century. Ordinary people are not using *line* loosely; on the contrary, geometry has borrowed an everyday word—one with dozens of valid meanings—to use in a narrow sense.

In for **Into.** "He was put in jail." "He went in the house." A man may be in jail, or be in a house, but when the act of entrance—the movement of something from the outside to the inside of another thing—is related the correct word is into if the latter thing is named.

. . .

Bierce's rule is the one we still learn in school: *Into* follows verbs of motion, *in* follows verbs of location. The problem is that since the dawn of English, there have been exceptions. When *in* and *into* divvied up the job previously done by the Old English dative and accusative cases, they didn't make a neat job of it by giving *in* the dative uses (it's *in* the car) and *into* the accusative ones (look *into* my eyes). Instead, many verbs whose meanings included motion, like *put*, *cast*, *fall*, and *throw*, were deemed not to need the sense of movement carried by *into*; they were paired with *in* instead. "I threw it *in* the river," "they laid him *in* a manger," "it broke *in* two," and Bierce's "wrong" example, "He was put in jail," are traditional, correct usage.

Inaugurate for **Begin, Establish,** etc. Inauguration implies some degree of formality and ceremony.

. . .

Inaugurate was defined as "begin" in Johnson's *Dictionary* (1755), but by the 19th century, critics heard the word as inflated journalese. Bryant 1870 banned its use in the *New York Evening Post*, and as late as the 1950s, Partridge's *Usage and Abusage* was calling it "grandiose and excessive." But formality is a relative judgment. *Inaugurate* still implies ceremony, but newspapers today report the inauguration of shipyards and prison chapels—uses that once might have sounded ludicrous even to critics less waspish than Bierce. See *Banquet, Preside*.

Incumbent for **Obligatory**. "It was incumbent upon me to re-lieve him." Infelicitous and work-worn. Say, It was my duty, or, if enamored of that particular metaphor, It lay upon me.

· · ·

Infelicity is in the eye of the beholder, and the prejudice against *incumbent* appears to be Bierce's own quirk. "Incumbent upon" is indeed a bit ponderous, and perhaps it was overused by the more high-flown writers of Bierce's generation, but it is perfectly standard—if even more ponderous-sounding—today.

Individual. As a noun, this word means something that cannot be considered as divided, a unit. But it is incorrect to call a man, woman or child an individual, except with reference to mankind, to society or to a class of persons. It will not do to say, "An indi-vidual stood in the street," when no mention nor allusion has been made, nor is going to be made, to some aggregate of indi-viduals considered as a whole.

· · ·

From the 1870s to 1920s, reports *MWDEU*, "it was fashionable to disparage *individual*" when used as a synonym for *person*. The ob-jections came partly on etymological grounds—as Bierce notes, "undividable" is the root sense of the word—and, perhaps, partly as a reaction to "journalistic overuse" of *individual* in facetious writing. In 1917, however, J. Lesslie Hall looked at the facts of usage and found that *individual* "was very popular with Coleridge, Hawthorne, Cooper, Dickens, Bulwer, Motley, and other distin-guished writers of the nineteenth century"—including Alexander Bain, the Scottish philosopher and eminent grammarian. Writers are still cautioned to avoid using *individual* for "person" unless that person is being singled out from a crowd; it can sound bureau-cratic and stilted. But some writers use it responsibly, says Garner 2003, and "they shouldn't have the word taken away from them."

Indorse. See **Endorse.**

Insane Asylum. Obviously an asylum cannot be unsound in mind. Say, asylum for the insane.

· · ·

In the mid-19th century, some people liked to argue that "grammatical error" was a nonsensical notion, because an error in language could not be "grammatical." Bierce's rejection of *insane asylum* is based on the same faulty logic. But such constructions are routine in English. Webster 1828 had an entry for the adjectival sense of *insane*: "Used by or appropriated to insane persons; as, an insane hospital." And Fitzedward Hall noted in 1872 that *insane asylum* was no more strange than *sickroom* or *madhouse*. As Garner 2003 points out, "criminal lawyer" and "logical fallacy" are similar phrases; any number of such pairs could be challenged as illogical by anyone trying hard enough to misunderstand them.

In Spite of. In most instances it is better to say despite.

· · ·

This is the judgment of a journalist, for whom brevity is the tiebreaker. But *in spite of* is older than, and synonymous with, *despite*. The choice is a matter of taste.

Inside of. Omit the preposition.

· · ·

Another journalistic whim. Except in expressions of time—"inside of a week, he'll be gone"—editors and teachers do, it's true, prefer *inside* (and *outside*) without the preposition: "I was inside the building, outside his office." Adding the *of* makes the phrase less formal, but as the journal *Inland and American Printer and Lithographer* conceded more than a century ago, in 1899, "'Inside of' is not strictly wrong." See *Outside of*.

Insignificant for Trivial, or Small. Insignificant means not signifying anything, and should be used only in contrast, expressed or implied, with something that is important for what it implies. The bear's tail may be insignificant to a naturalist tracing the animal's descent from an earlier species, but to the rest of us, not concerned with the matter, it is merely small.

• • •

Eric Partridge was still carrying this flag in the mid-20th century: "Insignificant does not mean 'small' but 'unimportant,'" he said in *Usage and Abusage*. Other critics seem to have ignored Bierce's fine distinction, perhaps rightly judging that it would be almost impossible to enforce. Bierce is correct that a scientist might call a bear's tail "insignificant," meaning something more specific than "small." But *insignificant* has several senses, and "small" has been one of them since the 1740s.

Insoluble for Unsolvable. Use the former word for material substances, the latter for problems.

• • •

Insoluble has been applied to bonds, relationships, and problems since the 14th century, and to non-dissolving materials since the 18th. *Unsolvable* (and *insolvable*) are later variations, now used only (as Bierce recommends) with respect to problems, not substances. There have been a few feeble efforts to impose the complete separation of senses Bierce is urging, but *insoluble* is really the only word you need.

Inst., Prox., Ult. These abbreviations of instante mense (in the present month), proximo mense (in the next month) and ultimo mense (in the last month), are serviceable enough in commercial correspondence, but, like A.M., P.M. and many other contractions of Latin words, could profitably be spared from literature.

• • •

For once we can say Bierce would be gratified to see what has become of us, a hundred years later. We never see *Inst.*, *Prox.*, or *Ult.* in literature. Why, we don't even see them in commercial correspondence—maybe the language isn't going to hell after all.

Integrity for **Honesty**. The word means entireness, wholeness. It may be rightly used to affirm possession of all the virtues, that is, unity of moral character.

· · ·

Bierce was not the only one who thought honesty a comparatively minimal virtue. George Crabb, in *English Synonymes* (1818), said, "People in general are denominated *honest* who pay what they owe, and do not adopt any methods of defrauding others: honesty in this sense, therefore, consists in negatives." Bierce (as usual) went further; in *The Devil's Dictionary*, he defined *honesty* as "Afflicted with an impediment in his dealing"—that is, unable to cheat.

Involve for **Entail**. "Proof of the charges will involve his dismissal." Not at all; it will entail it. To involve is, literally, to infold, not to bring about, nor cause to ensue. An unofficial investigation, for example, may involve character and reputation, but the ultimate consequence is entailed. A question, in the parliamentary sense, may involve a principle; its settlement one way or another may entail expense, or injury to interests. An act may involve one's honor and entail disgrace.

· · ·

Bierce thought *entail* was underused, but Henry Alford, nearly half a century earlier, had denounced the overuse of *entail* by English journalists seeking to sound important: "*Entail* is another poor injured verb. Nothing ever *leads to* anything as a consequence, or brings it about, but it always *entails* it. This smells strong of the lawyer's clerk."

Entail, to modern noses, still smells of the law office; except in formal contexts, we'd be more likely to say "will result in his dismissal" if *involve* seemed too vague.

It for So. "Going into the lion's cage is dangerous; you should not do it." Do so is the better expression, as a rule, for the word it is a pronoun, meaning a thing, or object, and therefore incapable of being done. Colloquially we may say do it, or do this, or do that, but in serious written discourse greater precision is desirable, and is better obtained, in most cases, by use of the adverb.

• • •

"Do so" is not really more precise than "do it," but it is more formal; it probably sounds even more elevated to contemporary Americans than it did to Bierce. There's a reason Nike didn't adopt the slogan "Just do so!"

Item for Brief Article. Commonly used of a narrative in a newspaper. Item connotes an aggregate of which it is a unit— one thing of many. Hence it suggests more than we may wish to direct attention to.

• • •

The use of *item* as a newspaper term dated from the early 19th century. Bryant put it on his "banned" list circa 1870; Schele de Vere included it in his 1871 book *Americanisms*, saying that the word "has in America the meaning of a point of information for the press. 'Local' reporters are forever in search of an item for their paper." Bierce's attempt at a joke—I think he means that calling news stories *items* suggests that they are mere repetitions of the same sort of thing—is not much of an argument, and his fellow journalists went right on collecting their *items*.

J

Jackies for **Sailors**. Vulgar, and especially offensive to seamen.

· · ·

The generic sailor had been styled "Jack Tar" since the 18th century—"Jack" for the ordinary man, the average Joe or John Doe, and "tar" for the stuff used to waterproof canvas on board. In the early days of the 20th century, it was not the nickname itself but the diminutive *jacky* that rankled. "This very objectionable term has obtained a certain vogue among the fresh young scribblers of the press," the *Sailor's Magazine and Seaman's Friend* editorialized in 1903. "It is . . . not only an outrage to the English language but an insult to the manhood of our sailors."

A letter to the *New York Times* in September 1905 blamed the press for reviving the word: "The recrudescence of 'jacky' in the past three years is to me inexplicable. The officers know the contemptuous character of the word, and they resent its use by newspapers even more than do the men." Most usage writers ignored the *jacky* dispute, but Bierce, a proud Civil War veteran, would have wanted his fellow journalists to get the message.

Jeopardize for **Imperil**, or **Endanger**. The correct word is jeopard, but in any case there is no need for anything so farfetched and stilted.

· · ·

Jeopardize was the "finalize" of the 19th century, "the object of the most heat and least rationality" among such verbs, says *MWDEU*. A swarm of usage mavens had already denounced *jeopardize* as monstrous, spurious, and intolerable before Bierce cast his vote; many of them, like Bierce, suggested reviving the near-extinct verb *jeopard*.

Fitzedward Hall was a voice of sanity in the din of derogation. "*Jeopardize*, however personally distasteful, is not a thing to vex one's soul about," he wrote in *Recent Exemplifications of False Philology* (1872). He even defended the suffix: "It is an advantage to language, as precluding ambiguity, that a verb should have a termination suggestive of its being a verb; and *-ize* is such a termination." The usage consensus went Hall's way; within a few years of Bierce's death, *jeopardize* was in all the dictionaries—and off the list of language controversies.

Juncture. Juncture means a joining, a junction; its use to signify a time, however critical a time, is absurd. "At this juncture the woman screamed." In reading that account of it we scream too.

· · ·

Not all of us scream at this *juncture*. Like his objection to using *space* for a period of time, Bierce's aversion to *juncture* is based on etymological literalism: He wants *juncture* to mean only a physical connection or joint. But the word had been used for a temporal joining—"a concurrence of events or circumstances"—since the mid-17th century. The *OED* quotes Pepys, whose *Diary* for June 30, 1662, recorded "as bad a juncture as ever I observed. The King and his new Queene minding their pleasures at Hampton Court. All people discontented."

Today some authorities advise limiting *juncture* to critical moments, and Microsoft's grammar checker flags the cliché "at this juncture," which Garner 2003 calls a pompous synonym for "now." But Bierce's opinion was roundly ignored; the temporal sense of *juncture* is now the dominant use.

Just Exactly. Nothing is gained in strength nor precision by this kind of pleonasm. Omit just.

· · ·

Bierce is suggesting that exactness has no degrees, but of course it has; your friend may be wearing the *same* shirt as you, or *exactly the same* shirt, or *just exactly the same* shirt. And if you've got a problem with your car's VIN, you may want to tell the inattentive clerk you need help with a "VIN number." Edited prose can often do without the extra cues, but in speech, emphasis does add precision, and a "superfluous" word or two may be just what the communication doctor ordered. See *And so, Later on, Self-confessed.*

Juvenile for **Child.** This needless use of the adjective for the noun is probably supposed to be humorous, like "canine" for dog, "optic" for eye, "anatomy" for body, and the like. Happily the offense is not very common.

• • •

The attacks on *juvenile* had begun half a century earlier, when Henry Alford, in *The Queen's English* (1864), accused British journalists of making pretentious substitutions—*party, female, juvenile*—for the plain Saxon *man, woman,* and *child.* Richard Meade Bache, in *Vulgarisms* (1869), made the same complaint of American newspaper prose: "A man is a *biped.* A woman is a *feminine.* A child is a *juvenile.* A dog is a *canine.* Fingers are *digits.*" But as Bierce recognized, the affectation was already on the wane. Soon enough, *juvenile* would be remanded to the custody of lawyers and psychologists, who rarely use the word with humorous intent.

K

Kind of a for **Kind of.** "He was that kind of a man." Say that kind of man. Man here is generic, and a genus comprises many kinds. But there cannot be more than one kind of one thing. Kind of followed by an adjective, as, "kind of good," is almost too gross for censure.

• • •

Goold Brown was apparently the first grammarian to articulate the logical objection to *kind of*, though he used the alternative *sort of* in his example: "Some will say, '*A jay* is a sort of *a bird*;' whereas they ought to say, '*The jay* is a sort of *bird*.' Because it is absurd to suggest, that one jay is a sort of one bird" (*The Grammar of English Grammars*, 1851).

But similar constructions had been around since the 14th century, says *MWDEU*; nobody had complained about Shakespeare's "a kind of a knave" or Fielding's "a good sort of a fellow." And even after Brown pointed out the logical flaw in the phrase, few critics adopted his reasoning. It was simpler just to call "a kind of a bird" wordy than to go into the whole genus-species thing.

As for *kind of good*, this adverbial *kind of* was about a century old when Bierce called it "gross." It had evolved naturally from the earlier uses of *kind of*, as the construction "He has a kind of obsession" morphed into "He's kind of obsessed." Vizetelly 1906 said, wrongly, that the phrase was "an American provincialism for *somewhat*"; usage writers ever since have been vaguely hostile to *kind of good*, for no particular reason.

L

Landed Estate for **Property in Land**. Dreadful!

• • •

What was so "dreadful" about *landed estate*? Since Bierce himself used *estate* to mean landholdings, it must have been *landed* that irked him. Perhaps he thought the adjective shared the taint of *talented*, a word universally denounced in Bierce's day because, like *landed*, it was formed from a noun, not a verb. (*To talent* and *to land* would have been proper ancestors, but those verbs didn't exist).

But *landed* had been grandfathered into the language; its use to mean "possessed of land" dates to the Laws of Athelstan in 1000, says the *OED*. Even *landed estate* was already at least two centuries old: Joseph Addison, in 1711, wrote in the *Spectator* that trade "has multiplied the Number of the Rich, made our Landed Estates infinitely more Valuable."

It's possible, though, that the issue wasn't the legitimacy of the word *landed* but the aura of privilege surrounding *landed estate*. Bierce was no socialist, but as a self-made man and lifelong renter, he had expressed a certain skepticism about private landholding. "Carried to its logical conclusion, it means that some have the right to prevent others from living," he wrote in *The Devil's Dictionary*. For "if the whole area of terra firma is owned by A, B and C, there will be no place for D, E, F and G to be born," and the unlanded masses will be exiled forever to life aboard ship—to "a home on the rolling deep."

Last and **Past**. "Last week." "The past week." Neither is accurate: a week cannot be the last if another is already begun; and all weeks except this one are past. Here two wrongs seem to make a right: we can say the week last past. But will we? I trow not.

. . .

Bierce pretends that *last* and *past* have only one sense, in order to prove them deficient. But he is faking it; he knows quite well that *last* can mean "most recent," not just "final," and that "the past week," with its definite article, is easily distinguished from all other past weeks. The usages were four or five centuries old already, and "accurate" enough for all but devoted nitpickers.

And even the nitpickers couldn't agree. Ayres 1896 allowed only *past*, never *last*, in phrases like "the past three days" and "the past

20 years." Ransom 1911 thought Ayres had it backward: "Every year, week or day since the creation and until the present is 'past.' What you mean is the year, week or day immediately preceding the present. Hence say precisely what you mean, which is 'last.'" No wonder Bierce wasn't sure what he thought about *last* and *past*.

Later on. On is redundant; say, later.

· · ·

Later on was relatively recent in Bierce's time, and in condemning it he was at the head of a parade that marched on (or limped on) through the first half of the 20th century. The detractors, of course, did not follow their own rule. Eric Partridge, in *Usage and Abusage* (1954), called *later on* "an uneconomical colloquialism." But in an essay on Henry Fielding, Partridge said the novelist "came into his own early in the Romantic period and more than kept his place later on." In another essay, he observed that "Later on, [King George III] almost lost his voice." Partridge the peevologist may have disapproved of *later on*, but Partridge the writer knew that economy isn't everything. See *And so, Self-confessed*.

Laundry. Meaning a place where clothing is washed, this word cannot mean, also, clothing sent there to be washed.

· · ·

Laundry as a word for the items being washed, not just the place of laundering, was a novelty when Bierce wrote. The usage may have started among students: A Rutgers fraternity handbook, dated 1893, advised new members, "Do not wear short pants, even when homesick, and under no circumstances hang your laundry on the Campus clothes-line."

But other nouns of *laundry*'s class had gone that way before, to the shock and horror of Richard Grant White. In *Words and Their Uses* (1870), White explained that *jewelry*, *crockery*, and *pottery*, which should refer to places, had been sadly corrupted. "The jew-eller put up JEWELRY over his shop door, and the crocker, CROCK-ERY, and so forth; and these names of places were at last misapprehended as names of the articles for sale in those places . . . *crockery* was the first, and is the best established, of these perverted words."

Clean linens weren't "articles for sale," but thanks to the spread of commercial laundries, they had become a kind of prod-uct as well; terms like *laundry list* and *laundry bag* no doubt en-couraged the transfer of the word *laundry* to the items on the lists and in the bags. And just as *jewelry* and *crockery* had turned into the names of objects, *laundry* soon became the standard word for washables.

Lay (to place) for **Lie** (to recline). "The ship lays on her side." A more common error is made in the past tense, as, "He laid down on the grass." The confusion comes of the identity of a present tense of the transitive verb to lay and the past tense of the in-transitive verb to lie.

• • •

Bierce diagnoses part of the problem—the similarity of *lay* and *laid*—but he probably doesn't know that *lay* had been used to mean *lie* for centuries before any grammarian noticed. One of the earliest objectors was Robert Baker, who offered an ingenious explanation for the confusion in *Remarks on the English Language* (1770): He thought contemporary writers were lazily imitating the French, who (he said) used *coucher* for both *lay* and *lie*. "These writers never employ the verb *to lie;* which I therefore suppose they would banish out of our language. 'The French make shift with one verb, and why should not we?' Most admirable reasoning, truly!"

Bierce's analysis of the confusion is more plausible, but he doesn't even hint at a solution. A century later, not much has changed: *Lie* and *lay* are still fairly well distinguished in edited prose; *lay* often takes the place of *lie* in speech; and usage watchers care as much as ever about getting it right.

Leading Question. A leading question is not necessarily an important one; it is one that is so framed as to suggest, or lead to, the answer desired. Few others than lawyers use the term correctly.

· · ·

A *leading question* can, of course, be an "important" question, when *leading* means "foremost": "Health care is the leading question." But Bierce is cautioning readers about the meaning of the legal *leading question*, which may have been a concern for journalists of his time. Today it's not a problem; after years of exposure to *Law & Order* reruns, most Americans will spot a leading question before the opposing attorney can yelp, "Objection!"

Lease. To say of a man that he leases certain premises leaves it doubtful whether he is lessor or lessee. Being ambiguous, the word should be used with caution.

· · ·

Lease had only turned ambiguous in the 19th century; unlike *rent*, which had meant both "let to a tenant" and "rent from a landlord" since the 16th century, *lease* had described what the owner did, not what the tenant did, for the previous six centuries. It's odd that Bierce is so restrained, merely urging caution when he might plausibly have fulminated over the new, sloppy use of *lease*.

Leave for **Go away.** "He left yesterday." Leave is a transitive verb; name the place of departure.

· · ·

"He left" seems uncontroversial now, but most of the 19th-century grammarians insisted that *leave* must have an object: "He left the hotel yesterday." The *OED*'s first example of the naked *leave*—Jeremy Bentham's "Lord L. . . . leaves on the 1st" (1791)—is labeled colloquial.

But if we know where Lord L. is leaving from, why does it have to be stated? A few brave usagists said it didn't; Henry Alford, in *The Queen's English* (1864), and Alfred Ayres, in *The Verbalist* (1881), thought "He left yesterday" was usually clear enough. A few decades into the 20th century, so did everyone else.

Leave for **Let.** "**Leave it alone.**" **By this many persons mean, not that it is to be left in solitude, but that it is to be untouched, or unmolested.**

• • •

"Leave it alone" meaning "let it alone," "don't disturb it," became widespread only in the later 19th century, says *MWDEU*, with the help of the well-known line about Little Bo-Peep's sheep: "Leave them alone, and they'll come home." The ensuing usage debate lasted into the 1980s, with some authorities continuing to insist on Bierce's distinction: "Let me alone" means "don't bother me," while "leave me alone" means "get out of my sight." Today, says Garner 2003, "only extreme purists will fault someone who uses *leave alone* in the nonliteral sense."

Lengthways for **Lengthwise.**

• • •

"American dictionaries give *endwise, lengthwise, side-wise*, as the preferred form," says Utter 1916, while "British usage seems to prefer the forms in *-ways*: *sideways, lengthways, endways*." Both versions of the words date to the 17th century, and both are acceptable, but Bierce liked his language consistent. It would have peeved him to find that we now prefer *sideways*, but *endwise*—and that *lengthwise* can go either way. See *Endways.*

Lengthy. Usually said in disparagement of some wearisome discourse. It is no better than breadthy, or thicknessy.

· · ·

Lengthy showed up in John Adams's diary ("I grow too minute and lengthy") in 1759, and though the British resisted the word, by 1788 it had appeared in *Gentleman's and London Magazine*, lending some metrical help to a bit of doggerel:

> *He tones like Pharisee sublime,*
> *Two lengthy prayers a-day.*

Bryant put *lengthy* on his list of banned words in 1870, but it was already too popular, on both sides of the Atlantic, to stamp out; most other critics didn't even try.

Leniency for Lenity. The words are synonymous, but the latter is the better.

· · ·

Leniency, formed from *lenience,* dates to the later 18th century; by the mid-19th it was upstaging the older word, *lenity,* convincingly enough to be included in American dictionaries. The usagists did not approve: Gould 1867 called *leniency* and *lenience* "two philological abortions," neither "properly constructed" nor needed, and most other commentators agreed. C. J. Smith, however, treated *leniency* as standard in his 1871 *Synonyms Discriminated,* and his was the view that prevailed.

Less for Fewer. "The regiment had less than five hundred men." Less relates to quantity, fewer, to number.

· · ·

Bierce, like many usage writers of his time and later, signs on to a "rule" that had not been enunciated (or observed) until the 18th century. Baker 1770 may have started the fad, by gently suggesting that "Fewer would do better" than *less*, and might be more elegant, with numbers.

In fact, as *MWDEU* notes, *less* had been used of countables since King Alfred the Great did it in 888, writing (in Old English) "with less words or with more." But Baker's preference was reinterpreted as a rule by later usagists, and in the 20th century it became a serious shibboleth.

Not every authority mindlessly saluted the rule. "There is no doubt that less than is treated as a plural [i.e., allowed in 'less than 20 were invited']," Bergen and Cornelia Evans wrote in *A Dictionary of Contemporary American Usage* (1957). "*Less* before a plural noun, as in *less men*, is not as widely accepted . . . But a great many [people] whose education and position cannot be questioned, see nothing wrong in it."

In practice, *less* is more often used than *fewer* when the number is thought of as a limit: A frying pan is "nine inches or less in diameter," for instance, because you aren't measuring in one-inch increments, just stating a maximum size. The same is true for Bierce's regiment: "Less than five hundred men," like "160 characters or less" for a text message, states an upper limit on a collection of countables; the countability isn't the point. It's a testament to our fondness for recreational nitpicking that so many of us think the *less*-vs.-*fewer* distinction is both rigid and important.

Liable for **Likely**. "Man is liable to err." Man is not liable to err, but to error. Liable should be followed, not by an infinitive, but by a preposition.

. . .

The critics of Bierce's day worked hard at fine-tuning the uses of *liable*, *likely*, and *apt*, but the notion that *liable* could not be followed by an infinitive seems to be Bierce's own hallucination. In fact, the construction had been in use for more than two centuries:

"All would be liable to die," wrote Thomas Creech, a British scholar, in 1682, and writers ever since have followed his example. See *Apt, Likely*.

Like for As, or As if. "The matter is now like it was." "The house looked like it would fall."

· · ·

Long before "Winston tastes good like a cigarette should" scandalized the nation, *like* as a conjunction, instead of *as* or *as if*, was a worry to usage mavens. But it has long been common in speech, and some variations are widely accepted. *The American Heritage Guide to Contemporary Usage,* for instance, says conjunctive *like* is fine "with verbs such as *feel, look, seem, sound,* and *taste*." That makes Bierce's second "bad" example standard 21st-century prose. As for all the other *like*s, proper usage depends on your ear and your editor.

Likely for Probably. "He will likely be elected." If likely is thought the better word (and in most cases it is) put it this way: "It is likely that he will be elected," or, "He is likely to be elected."

· · ·

Bierce seems to be the first critic to protest the use of *likely* as a solo adverb; he is responding to change in usage that had unfolded over the 19th century.

From the 14th century into the 19th, it was normal to write "you're likely correct," or—as usage critic Albert N. Raub did in 1897—"it will likely rain to-night." By the turn of the century, though, idiom had begun to demand that *likely* have a modifier: "He'll likely win" was a bit suspect, but "He'll very likely win" was fine.

Some 20th-century usagists, especially the *New York Times*'s Theodore Bernstein, tried to make that tendency into a rule, but they never quite killed off the "he'll likely win" construction. In the past twenty years, it has been coming back into print use, and by now it probably sounds normal to most Americans. Not to Bill Bryson, however; in a fit of nostalgia or Anglophilia, he included *likely* in his 2008 *Bryson's Dictionary for Writers and Editors*. "Used as an adverb," he says, "*likely* needs to be accompanied by one of four helping words: *very, quite, more,* or *most*." Judging by the print evidence, writers and editors are not rushing to heed that advice.

Limited for **Small, Inadequate,** etc. "The army's operations were confined to a limited area." "We had a limited supply of food." A large area and an adequate supply would also be limited. Everything that we know about is limited.

• • •

Literalism strikes again. Yes, everything we know about is limited, except for eternity and infinity. So if we couldn't use *limited* in a relative sense—as we also use *big, small, warm,* and *cold*—there would be no reason to use it at all. A "limited" supply of food is, of course, one that might run out inconveniently soon. The trickle of complaints about *limited* had begun by the 1880s, and it didn't finally dry up till the 1960s. But *limited* in the sense of "circumscribed" had a long head start on its enemies. The usage had appeared in a 1610 commentary on the Book of Daniel by the English divine Andrew Willet: "The knowledge of angels is limited."

Line for **Kind,** or **Class.** "This line of goods." Leave the word to "salesladies" and "salesgentlemen." "That line of business." Say, that business.

• • •

Boswell reports that Samuel Johnson tried to "repress colloquial barbarisms . . . such as *line*, for *department*, or *branch*, as the civil line, the banking line." But the "line of business" notion is drawn from the King James Bible (1611), where Paul, in 2 Corinthians 10:16, speaks of "another man's line of things." English scholars had used the phrase throughout the 17th century; Johnson's objections were too little, too late.

"Line of goods" came later, but it was familiar enough by 1825 to show up in the dialogue of a novel called *Marriage*: "This line of goods is not easily transported about." Both expressions are still mainly commercial language, but we're too busy despising *incent* and *leverage* to worry about little old *line*.

Literally for **Figuratively**. "The stream was literally alive with fish." "His eloquence literally swept the audience from its feet." It is bad enough to exaggerate, but to affirm the truth of the exaggeration is intolerable.

• • •

Nonliteral uses of *literally* show up in Dryden (1687) and in Pope (1708), who wrote, "Every day with me is literally another yesterday for it is exactly the same." This intensifying use of *literally* passed unnoticed by critics; it was the 19th-century hyperbolic use of the term—especially with nonliteral images, as in Dickens's "he had literally feasted his eyes"—that drove the 20th-century mavens mad.

In 1903, the *L* volume of the *OED* appeared, with a usage note on *literally*: "Now often improperly used to indicate that some conventional metaphorical or hyperbolical phrase is to be taken in the strongest admissible sense." According to *MWDEU*, the quotation that prompted the note was from actress Fanny Kemble in 1863: "For the last four years . . . I literally coined money." The hyperbolic usage is not, says *MWDEU*, "a mistake for *figuratively*," but a natural extension of the intensive use; it isn't wrong, but "hyperbole requires care in handling" if it's not to sound ludicrous.

Jesse Sheidlower, editor at large of the *OED*, made the same point in a 2005 *Slate* magazine article. A blanket condemnation of *literally*, he said, would be as extreme as banning the unreal *really* that Meg uses in *Little Women*: "It's been such a dismal day I'm really dying for some amusement." The point is to avoid silly writing, not to avoid *literally*.

That's the consensus of the *American Heritage Dictionary*, too. In the latest survey, 66 percent of the *AHD* usage panel accepted the intensive *literally* ("They had literally no help"); 37 percent allowed *literally* with a "dead metaphor" ("literally out of his mind"); but only 23 percent approved "literally swallowing the country's youth." So lovers of *literally* need to watch their step, figuratively speaking.

Loan for Lend. "I loaned him ten dollars." We lend, but the act of lending, or, less literally, the thing lent, is a loan.

· · ·

Loan was an old English verb, though not so old as *lend*, that came to the colonies with the settlers. It eventually fell out of use in Britain, but persisted in America: "It is charged . . . that officers of the Bank have loaned money at usurious rates," said Lincoln in an 1837 speech.

But when the American literati realized that *loan* was no longer good British English, they began to denounce it. White 1870 declared it "wrong: not a verb but a noun," a canard that teachers and journalists—and even the *New York Times* stylebook—repeat even today. White imagined that *loan* was intended to impress, as did Ayres 1881: "Only those having a vulgar *penchant* for big words . . . will prefer [*loan*] to its synonym *lend*," Ayres said. Why *loan* would qualify as pretentious—or as "big"!—neither man tried to explain.

Locate. "After many removals the family located at Smithville." Some dictionaries give locate as an intransitive verb having that meaning, but—well, dictionaries are funny.

· · ·

"*Locate* is a common Americanism, insufferable to ears at all sensitive," said White 1870. "If a gentleman chooses to say, 'I guess I shall locate in Muzzouruh,' meaning that he thinks he shall settle in Missouri, he has, doubtless, the right, as a free and independent citizen of the United States, to say so." The "vulgarism" was apparently common in newspapers of the time: "Dr. and Mrs. Ambrose Foster left Evanston for their annual winter trip to the South," reported the *Chicago Tribune* in 1875. "They will locate at Atlanta, Ga." The usage has ebbed, however, and is now mostly restricted to businesses: A Costco may *locate* in Dubuque, but an ordinary person simply moves there.

Lots, or a **Lot**, for **Much**, or **Many**. "Lots of things." "A lot of talk."

· · ·

Lots, said Vizetelly 1906, is "A slipshod colloquialism for 'great many,'" and thus "to be avoided, as are all other vague, ill-assigned expressions, as tending to indistinctness of thought." Informal it may be, but *lots* is surely no more "vague" or "indistinct" than Bierce's preferred *much* and *many*.

Love for **Like**. "I love to travel." "I love apples." Keep the stronger word for a stronger feeling.

· · ·

Since Bierce defined *love* as "A temporary insanity curable by marriage," he's not the most credible authority on liking and loving. This distinction was a popular one among 19th-century grammarians, however, as it offered an excellent opportunity to moralize. "One may, without shame, say that he loves books, that he loves the Fine Arts, that he loves Nature," said Richard Meade Bache in *Vulgarisms* (1869). But "one cannot with propriety speak of loving food. If persons really mean what they say, when they speak of loving oysters, cake, ice-cream, etc., it is confessing a deplorable circumstance, which they would do better to keep to themselves."

Richard Grant White told readers how lucky they were to have a choice of verbs: "It gives us an advantage over the French . . . who are obliged to use the same word to express their affection for *La France* and for *méringues à la crème*. We shall have deteriorated, as well as our language, when we no longer distinguish our liking from our loving" (*Words and Their Uses*, 1870).

Lectures on this theme continued well into the 20th century, though critics never did agree on what exactly (besides God, family, and country) it was permissible to "love." "Happily, all this nonsense has blown over," says *MWDEU*. "You can use *love* for trivial occasions ('I'd love to go bowling but I have to do my income tax') or important ones ('I love my wife') without confusing or revolting anyone."

Lunch for Luncheon. But do not use luncheon as a verb.

• • •

Bierce's opposition to *lunch* as a noun came late in the game. The first mention of the meal in the *OED* comes from Henry Digby Beste's "Remarks on Popular Etymology," published in an 1829 collection. "The word *lunch* is adopted in that 'glass of fashion,' Almacks [a popular London club]," said Beste, "and *luncheon* is avoided as unsuitable to the polished society there exhibited." Not everyone admired the new fashion; Alfred Ayres, in *The Verbalist* (1881), called *lunch* "an inelegant abbreviation," and Robert W. Ransom, an editor at the *Chicago Record-Herald*, banned it as a colloquialism in his 1911 usage guide. But their efforts were in vain: Robert Palfrey Utter, echoing the *OED*, admitted in 1916 that "As a noun, *lunch* is now the usual word."

M

Mad for **Angry**. An Americanism of lessening prevalence. It is probable that anger is a kind of madness (insanity), but that is not what the misusers of the word mad mean to affirm.

• • •

Mad was not, in fact, an Americanism. Webster 1828 noted that *mad* for "angry" was "thus used by [Pope's friend John] Arbuthnot, and is perfectly proper." In *Americanisms* (1871), Maximilian Schele de Vere called *mad* "excellent old English" and cited a number of British examples, including a 1663 exchange from Pepys's *Diary*: "Said I: 'Sister, while I was preaching, did you get *mad*?' She answered: 'Yes, very *mad*; I could have cut your throat.'" And Alfred Ayres, in *The Verbalist* (1881), defended *mad* with quotes from Shakespeare and the Bible. These facts made no difference to Bierce and his *mad*-hating successors, the schoolteachers who kept trying to tell us—against the evidence of our ears and eyes—that *mad* could only mean "insane," never "angry."

Maintain for **Contend**. "The senator maintained that the tariff was iniquitous." He maintained it only if he proved it.

• • •

Not for the first time, I ask myself: Where did Bierce get this stuff? *Maintain* meaning "defend a position, assert" dates to the 14th century, and *maintaining* a position has never required "proving" it. The *OED*'s examples include "He . . . Maintains the Multitude can never err" (Dryden, 1682) and "The Epicureans . . . maintained that absence of pain was the highest happiness" (Bishop Joseph Butler, 1729)—both instances where proof would be unlikely if not impossible.

Majority for **Plurality**. Concerning votes cast in an election, a majority is more than half the total; a plurality is the excess of one candidate's votes over another's. Commonly the votes compared are those for the successful candidate and those for his most nearly successful competitor.

. . .

Bierce is not distinguishing, as most usage books do, between a winning *majority* (more than half the votes cast) and a *plurality* (the largest number, but less than half). He is grinding a different ax: He objects to the use of *majority*, rather than *plurality*, to describe a margin of victory. But *majority* had been used to mean the margin throughout Bierce's lifetime: "The latter won by a majority of 816 in a total vote of 2810," the *New York Times* reported on August 29, 1900. The usage is no longer common in the United States—belatedly, we've taken Bierce's advice—but it's still current in Britain and other countries.

Make for **Earn**. "He makes fifty dollars a month by manual labor."

. . .

Perhaps Bierce thought "make money" was a cornpone Americanism, as others did, but it's not so. Boswell, notes *MWDEU*, thought the phrase "make money" was "pretty current," though Johnson rebuked him for using it (*Life of Johnson*, 1791). The *OED* cites an example of "make money" from the late 15th century, and the expression appears in Shakespeare, Jane Austen, and Melville. There's nothing wrong with "making" money.

Mansion for **Dwelling**, or **House**. Usually mere hyperbole, a lamentable fault of our national literature. Even our presidents, before Roosevelt, called their dwelling the Executive Mansion.

. . .

Mansion is an old and respectable word, and some of Bierce's contemporaries thought *mansion* and *residence* were fine names for
what Utter 1916 called "a house of a superior kind." But the times
were changing, and Bierce was on the anti-bombast bandwagon.
Just a few years later, in the first edition of her classic *Etiquette*
(1922), Emily Post would explain to Americans that in "the best society," the person who owns a mansion calls it a house, just as she
keeps not a "chauffeur" and "limousine," but a car and driver.

The president's house, as Bierce says, was often called the Executive Mansion (as it still is informally) until 1901. According to
the official White House Web site, Theodore Roosevelt changed
it by the simple act of having his stationery engraved with "The
White House."

Masculine for **Male**. See *Feminine*.

Meet for **Meeting**. This belongs to the language of sport, which
persons of sense do not write—nor read.

· · ·

Meet was indeed new as a slang term for an athletic competition,
but the word had been a colloquial form of *meeting* for a century.
Probably Bierce just took this as an opportunity to cock a snook at
sportswriters, whom he ranked even lower than ordinary journalists.

Mend for **Repair**. "They mended the road." To mend is to repair, but to repair is not always to mend. A stocking is mended,
a road repaired.

· · ·

True, *mend* and *repair* are not completely interchangeable, but
Bierce gives no clue to how we would choose between them. That's
because the choice is a matter of changing custom, not fixed rule.
The *OED*'s citations for *mend*, which date to about 1225, mention
the mending of churches, windows, ships, pens, and ditches; by

Bierce's time there's also lots of indoor mending, of clothing, furniture, and household items. It's not a sharp distinction, nor a usage anyone is likely to get wrong.

Militate. "Negligence militates against success." If "militate" meant anything it would mean fight, but there is no such word.

· · ·

In the 1600s, says the *OED*, *militate* did indeed mean literally to fight as a soldier, as well as "campaign, strive" and "contradict." Webster 1828 defined it as "to oppose; to be or to act in opposition." Bierce may be taking his cue from Richard Grant White, who called *militate* "absurd" and one "among words which are not words" (*Words and Their Uses*, 1870). Bierce and White were mistaken.

Mind for **Obey.** This is a reasonless extension of one legitimate meaning of mind, namely, to heed, to give attention.

· · ·

Actually, it's not much of an extension from the "pay attention" sense of *mind*—the *OED*'s earliest example is "If men wolde diligently mind St. Paul's wordes" (1559)—to "mind what your mother says" and then to "mind your mother." The "obey" sense had appeared, along with other meanings of *mind*, in Webster 1828. But when Alfred Ayres finally noticed it, late in the century, he was not pleased. In the 1896 edition of *The Verbalist*, he called it inelegant, if not incorrect, and urged separation of the two meanings: "*Mind* [pay attention to] what I say, and be sure you *obey* me." Most usagists ignored his plea, but his advice would have appealed to Bierce, the constant weeder and pruner of the lexicon.

Minus for **Lacking,** or **Without.** "After the battle he was minus an ear." It is better in serious composition to avoid such alien words as have vernacular equivalents.

· · ·

Avoid it "in serious composition," the killjoys always say, but they never explain how serious is too serious for any given word. In 1907 the *OED* called this sense of *minus* a "chiefly colloquial" use; today, says *MWDEU*, it is a bit informal, but often used "in serious, if not highly solemn, writing." Would a "highly solemn" writer even be tempted to say "minus an ear"? If the answer is no, we are minus one usage problem.

Mistaken for **Mistake**. "You are mistaken." For whom? Say, You mistake.

. . .

"He was mistaken for a burglar" means one thing; "he thought you were a burglar, but he was mistaken" means quite another. Both uses date to the 16th century or earlier, though, and the one Bierce disapproves of—"to be in error"—is the older.

Some tidy-minded usagists were naturally annoyed by a phrase that could mean either "you are misunderstood" or "you misunderstand." Gould 1867 called the older, "you're wrong" sense "one of the most widely disseminated of philological errors." Ayres 1896 passed along a defense of it from a "learned friend" who explained, " 'You are mistaken' is a euphemism for 'You are wrong'; it has less offensiveness."

In practice, *mistaken* ("in error") and *mistaken for* cause no confusion at all. And Bierce could not have taken the debate very seriously; in *The Devil's Dictionary*, he used *mistaken* in the "wrong" sense, defining *positive* as "Mistaken at the top of one's voice."

Monarch for **King, Emperor,** or **Sovereign**. Not only hyperbolical, but inaccurate. There is not a monarch in Christendom.

. . .

Bierce is saying that *monarch* properly means "absolute ruler," and the postrevolutionary sovereigns of his era fall far short of that description. But the word had long been used as a variant of *sovereign*, *queen*, *ruler*, and other such terms, as Bierce the journalist surely knew.

He elaborated on the plight of monarchs in *The Devil's Dictionary*: "In Russia and the Orient the monarch has still a considerable influence in public affairs and in the disposition of the human head, but in western Europe political administration is mostly entrusted to his ministers, he being somewhat preoccupied with reflections relating to the status of his own head."

Moneyed for **Wealthy.** "The moneyed men of New York." One might as sensibly say, "The cattled men of Texas," or, "The lobstered men of the fish market."

. . .

Most of Bierce's fellow usagists considered *moneyed* just as acceptable as *whiskered*, *lettered*, *cloistered*, and *anguished*, which were also based on nouns, not verbs. But Bierce lumps *moneyed* with *talented*, which was a newer coinage, still regarded by some as illegitimate. (*To money*, in fact, had been a verb—as late as 1854, Thackeray wrote of "the banker who moneys me"—but the adjective came first.) See *Landed*, *Talented*.

Most for **Almost.** "The apples are most all gone." "The returning travelers were most home."

. . .

Most for "almost" has two different uses; the one Bierce cites is "dialectal or old-fashioned," according to *MWDEU*, which quotes Huckleberry Finn's "It most froze me." The other, used with words like *everyone*, *anyone*, and *all*, is standard American, though informal: "He competes most every Saturday." It's a fair bet, though, that Bierce would have loathed them equally.

Moved for **Removed.** "The family has moved to another house." "The Joneses were moving."

• • •

In *Americanisms* (1848), John Russell Bartlett quoted a New York newspaper mocking the use of *move*: "These are great *moving* times . . . Could the sovereigns of Europe only *move* as easily as the sovereigns of New York do, from house to house, palace to palace, &c., they would be well content."

But *moved* had been challenging the older *removed*, even in England, for two hundred years. Defoe, in 1722, used both verbs in a single sentence to describe a change of residence: "With this certificate they removed, though with great reluctance; . . . they moved towards the marshes on the side of Waltham." Webster 1828 listed both *move* and *remove* in this sense: "Men move with their families from one house, town or state to another." Both words were current in Bierce's time; he simply backed the wrong horse.

Mutual. By this word we express a reciprocal relation. It implies exchange, a giving and taking, not a mere possessing in common. There can be a mutual affection, or a mutual hatred, but not a mutual friend, nor a mutual horse.

• • •

The *mutual* debate is a mystifyingly persistent tradition. The idea that *mutual* can't mean "common" was never truly a rule, and has never been obeyed, yet in 2003, Garner's *Modern American Usage* could say flatly that "whatever is mutual is reciprocal—it's directed by each toward the other."

But that rule—Bierce's rule—rests on a wobbly 18th-century foundation. First, as *MWDEU* explains, Samuel Johnson failed to note the "common" sense of *mutual* in his *Dictionary* (1755), even though it had been current since 1600. In fact, Johnson's own illustrative quotation, from Shakespeare, used *mutual* in the "common" sense, describing a herd of wild animals: "If . . . any air of music touch their ears, You shall perceive them make a mutual stand."

Then Robert Baker, in his 1770 book *Remarks on the English Language*, told readers that *mutual* was "often improperly employed"; it could only mean "reciprocal," he said. "It would be absurd [to call a third person] *Our mutual Benefactor*. The proper Expression would be *Our common Benefactor*."

Did writers obey? They did not. Fitzedward Hall, in 1873, quoted Laurence Sterne, Edmund Burke, Robert Southey, Disraeli, and Dickens—not just in the title *Our Mutual Friend* but also in *The Pickwick Papers*—using the forbidden *mutual*. Webster 1913 didn't like "our mutual friend," but admitted that the word was thus used "by many writers of high authority." And *mutual* continues to thrive, perhaps because the "correct" alternative, *common*, can be ambiguous: Is our common friend someone we both know, or someone who spits on the sidewalk?

The usage mavens, however, seem committed to their *mutual* resistance. It seems like a lot of fretting to lavish on a tiny, not really wrong, and never misleading usage variant. But somewhere, Ambrose Bierce is smiling.

N

Name for **Title and Name.** "His name was Mr. Smith." Surely no babe was ever christened Mister.

• • •

Bierce's problem with "Mr. Smith" is similar to his problem with *née*, and similarly obscure; the only other reference to it I could turn up was in *Irvine's Dictionary of Titles* (1912): "Mr. John Jones was born plain baby Jones . . . His name, to which he was born, is Jones, but his title is *Mr.* This is a fine distinction, but a distinction nevertheless." Fine it is, but is it useful? "His name is Mr. X" was once common in literature, often in the speech of characters who could not plausibly have said "His name is Smith." And as nobody was likely to adopt the wording "His title and name are Mr. and Smith," this fine distinction went straight to peeve heaven. See *Née.*

Necessaries for Means. "Bread and meat are necessaries of life." Not so; they are the mere means, for one can, and many do, live comfortably without them. Food and drink are necessaries of life, but particular kinds of food and drink are not.

• • •

Necessaries and *necessities* (below) are overlapping terms that the 19th-century word wrestlers tried mightily to pry apart. They wanted *necessaries* to mean air, water, food, and shelter—the minimum requirements for survival. Everything else, from chocolate cake to white truffles, might be a "necessity"—a habitual craving—to someone.

Bierce wanted to take this fundamentalism even further, apparently, and ban metonymies such as *bread* and *meat* for "food"; anything that specific went into its own category called "means." His fellow Americans saw a simpler way: They ignored *means*, dropped *necessaries* entirely, and made *necessities* the general word. This preference, noted Evans and Evans 1957, "may have been influenced by the fact that until recently a *necessary* was a euphemism in many rural areas for a privy or a chamberpot."

Necessities for Necessaries. "Necessities of life are those things without which we cannot live."

• • •

For Americans, this distinction was neither a necessity nor a necessary. See, if you must, *Necessaries*.

Née. Feminine of né, born. "Mrs. Jones, née Lucy Smith." She could hardly have been christened before her birth. If you must use the French word say, née Smith.

· · ·

Here is that rare case where technology rather than custom has made a language proscription obsolete. Since the advent of prenatal ultrasound, many children are named—though not "christened"—before birth. (And that "christened" is rather loose usage for a precisian like Bierce; he certainly knew people could have names without being baptized.)

Né does mean born, in French, but it's been compromised and hybridized in English. We sometimes use it to mean "former," especially in jokey contexts like the *OED*'s example from *U.S. News* (2001): "Chilean sea bass (née Patagonian toothfish) have been virtually eliminated from much of their range."

Negotiate. From the Latin negotium. It means, as all know, to fix the terms for a transaction, to bargain. But when we say, "The driver negotiated a difficult turn of the road," or, "The chauffeur negotiated a hill," we speak nonsense.

· · ·

Negotiate meaning "maneuver" was a recent sense of the verb, first recorded in 1862 in an English reference to fox hunting, and imported to America by the turn of the century. H. W. Fowler, in *The King's English* (1906), explained why the coinage must have come from those boring horsy folks: "People whose conversation runs much upon a limited subject feel the need of new phrases for the too familiar things."

Bierce was in the vanguard of American opposition to the new sense of *negotiate*. We don't know where he saw the verb, or why he disliked it; maybe novelty was its only crime. But it's possible he also noticed that his younger rival, fellow San Franciscan Jack London, was fond of using the word.

Neither—or for **Neither—nor.** "Neither a cat or fish has wool." Always after neither use nor.

. . .

This advice to pair *neither* and *nor* is universal and almost universally followed. There are, however, deviations, like Byron's "I neither ride or shoot." If you, like Byron, should use an *or* with *neither*, "you will have committed no dreadful solecism," says *MWDEU*. Bierce would have begged to differ; he thought (or pretended to think) that using *neither* with *or* changed the sense entirely. For his tortured reasoning, see *Or*.

New Beginner for **Beginner.**

. . .

It's not obvious why *new beginner*, a garden-variety redundancy, was singled out for censure. And yet the whole pack of snarling peeve-hunters fell upon the phrase, with Richard Meade Bache in the lead. "One may, after having failed in an attempt, make a *new beginning*, and analogy may perhaps be strained so far as to permit us to consider such a person, on a renewal of his attempt, a *new beginner*," he wrote in *Vulgarisms* (1869). "But it is unreasonable, although not unusual, to apply the phrase to one who is beginning for the *first* time."

As Bache admitted, *new beginner* was not unusual. Several 18th-century dictionaries, in fact, defined *novice* as "new beginner," and Swift used the expression in his "Letter to a Young Gentleman Lately Entered into Holy Orders" (1720). Since *beginner* had another definition—"founder, inciter, originator"—perhaps *new beginner* was a way to distinguish the two senses. Or maybe, in an era of long apprenticeships, *new beginner* was used to identify the greenest of the greenhorns. At any rate, either the redundancy or the complaining (or both) has now subsided.

Nice for **Good**, or **Agreeable**. "A nice girl." Nice means fastidious, delicately discriminative, and the like. Pope uses the word admirably of a dandy who was skilled in the nice conduct (management) of a clouded cane.*

· · ·

Nice has had many, many senses over the centuries besides "fastidious," including "foolish," "wanton," "ostentatious," "slothful," and "shy." The one Bierce and his many allies were resisting, however, was our current sense of *nice*—"agreeable, pleasant"—which had taken off in the mid-18th century. Jane Austen both used it and satirized it in *Northanger Abbey* (1818):

> "I am sure," cried Catherine, "I did not mean to say any thing wrong; but it is a nice book, and why should not I call it so?"
>
> "Very true," said Henry, "and this is a very nice day, and we are taking a very nice walk, and you are two very nice young ladies. Oh! it is a very nice word indeed!—it does for every thing."

Austen mocked, Bierce squawked, but everyone else has taken Catherine's side: *Nice* does do for everything! Henry Alford used it in *The Queen's English* (1864), saying that names like Jack and Ned were "not half so nice as the names which they have superseded." *MWDEU* quotes Faulkner, Frost, Hemingway, and Thurber using *nice;* the *OED* cites Dickens, Hardy, and Lawrence. The fact that

---

* Pope's "clouded cane" belongs to Sir Plume in *The Rape of the Lock* (1714). Brewer's *Dictionary of Phrase and Fable* (1898) defines it as "a malacca cane clouded or mottled from age and use." However, the definition of *cloud* in Webster 1913—"to variegate with colors" or other markings—suggests that faux clouding was also a possibility.

fourth-graders overuse the word in book reports should not deter adults from using *nice*, whose genial vagueness is so often exactly what one wants in an adjective.

No Use. "He tried to smile, but it was no use." Say, *of no use*, or, less colloquially, *in vain*.

. . .

The usage mavens appear to have noticed the abbreviated *no use* only around 1900, when it had been spreading for about a century. It wasn't the only phrase getting streamlined: "A dozen of eggs" had been trimmed to "a dozen eggs," and "this side of the pond" was replacing "on this side." Citizens and critics adapted to these changes, but *no use* stuck in some craws; Partridge's *Usage and Abusage* labeled it "incorrect—or, at best, colloquial" as late as the mid-1950s. Today the older form is barely remembered. And in sentences like "There's no use crying about it," as Garner 2003 notes, "the longer phrase, *of no use*, would be of no use . . . unless [such] sentences were rearranged—and made slightly longer."

Noise for Sound. "A noise like a flute"; "a noise of twittering birds," etc. A noise is a loud or disagreeable sound, or combination or succession of sounds.

. . .

If Bierce thought that bird sounds were never "noise," his avian neighbors must have been unusually melodious. It's true, as he says, that *noise* is generally unpleasant or disturbing sounds. But the word was used of pleasant sounds for centuries, and even now it can be neutral, as in the joke about attracting the Easter bunny: "Hide in a bush and make a noise like a carrot."

None. Usually, and in most cases, singular; as, None has come. But it is not singular because it always means not one, for frequently it does not, as, The bottle was full of milk, but none is left. When it refers to numbers, not quantity, popular usage stubbornly insists that it is plural, and at least one respectable authority says that as a singular it is offensive. One is sorry to be offensive to a good man.

. . .

Bierce did not learn his *none*-is-singular rule from any of the usage books—because none of the grammarians before him, scholarly or popular, had endorsed that rule. They all noted that *none* was both singular and plural, and had been for a long time.

In fact, nobody knows where this myth came from. According to *MWDEU*'s account, Lindley Murray may have planted the seed by observing, in 1795, that *none* was formed from the words *ne an*, "not one." That didn't mean *none* was singular: Even in Old English, it was both singular and plural. But it may have given the singular-*none* myth just enough credence to ensure its spread among certainty-seeking schoolteachers and journalists.

Thomas Lounsbury, author of *The Standard of Usage in English* (1908), didn't know where the folklore had begun, but he thought it was nuts. "There is no harm in a man's limiting his employment of *none* to the singular in his own individual usage, if he derives any pleasure from this particular form of linguistic martyrdom," he wrote. "But why should he go about seeking to inflict upon others the misery which owes its origin to his own ignorance?"

Novel for **Romance.** In a novel there is at least an apparent attention to considerations of probability; it is a narrative of what might occur. Romance flies with a free wing and owns no allegiance to likelihood. Both are fiction, both works of imagination, but should not be confounded. They are as distinct as beast and bird.

. . .

As readers of Bierce's stranger tales might guess, he classes himself with the birds of romance, not the beasts of realism. Realistic fiction is an inferior, earthbound genre, he says—"mere reporting" of what might have happened. " 'Probability'—which is but another name for the commonplace—is its keynote," he wrote in an 1897 essay. "Do these little fellows, the so-called realists, ever think of the goodly company which they deny themselves by confining themselves to their clumsy feet and pursuing their stupid noses through the barren hitherland, while just beyond the Delectable Mountains lies in light the Valley of Dreams, with its tall immortals, poppy-crowned?"

Numerous for **Many**. Rightly used, numerous relates to numbers, but does not imply a great number. A correct use is seen in the term numerous verse—verse consisting of poetic numbers; that is, rhythmical feet.

· · ·

Bierce's offhand treatment of the first *numerous* suggests that he just wants an excuse to flaunt the technical term "numerous verse," the style of verse he himself wrote. But the other *numerous* was the problematic one. Ayres 1896, unlike Bierce, thought it did imply "a great number," but he wanted it used only with collective nouns: "A numerous acquaintance" was allowable, or "a numerous family." On second thought, he mused, "large is usually—perhaps always:—the better word to use." There was a good reason for his waffling; *numerous acquaintances* was just as proper as *a numerous acquaintance*, and had been for three hundred years.

O

Obnoxious for **Offensive**. Obnoxious means exposed to evil. A soldier in battle is obnoxious to danger.

· · ·

If *obnoxious* in the sense "exposed to harm" had been current when Bierce was writing, his stubborn loyalty to it might be understandable. But it was more than halfway out the door. It had been displaced by the current meaning, "highly unpleasant," which was no rude upstart; the *OED*'s earliest example of it dates to 1675.

Occasion for Induce, or Cause. "His arrival occasioned a great tumult." As a verb, the word is needless and unpleasing.

· · ·

A personal quirk of Bierce's, apparently. *Occasion* meaning "give rise to, cause, bring about" dates to the mid-15th century, and a number of writers—including usage critics from Alford 1864 to Garner 2003—have found it both needful and pleasing.

Occasional Poems. These are not, as so many authors and compilers seem to think, poems written at irregular and indefinite intervals, but poems written for occasions, such as anniversaries, festivals, celebrations and the like.

· · ·

If Bierce accused the common folk of misunderstanding *occasional poetry*, his charge might be credible. (These days, of course, the media thoroughly reeducate us whenever a major "occasional" work—like the poem for Inauguration Day 2009—is commissioned.) But is it likely that the "authors and compilers" of Bierce's acquaintance thought occasional poems were verses "written at irregular intervals"? No doubt this *occasional* is occasionally confusing, but Bierce's suggestion that it baffled his fellow literati sounds more like a gibe than a fact.

Of Any for Of All. "The greatest poet of any that we have had."

· · ·

Lindley Murray, in *An English Grammar* (1809), explained that this form of the superlative was flawed: "We should not say, 'The best of any man' . . . for 'the best of men.'" Reasonable enough, when you look at his short example, and later usagists seconded his opinion. But "the best book of any I've read this summer" has been idiomatic English since Chaucer, as *MWDEU* notes. Modern editors, indoctrinated by Murray's followers, may be weeding it out, but the usage remains "old, well-established, and standard."

Offhanded and **Offhandedly.** Offhand is both adjective and adverb; these are bastard forms.

· · ·

The bastard *offhanded* is now legitimate, but it doesn't do anything *offhand* can't do. *Offhandedly* is a different story; it was new in the 19th century, but it isn't just another form of *offhand*; it has a job of its own.

"*Offhand* is [usually] a sentence modifier which basically means 'without premeditation or preparation,'" says *MWDEU*, which provides an example from the *New Yorker*: "Offhand, I'd say that there will be at least nine starters."

Offhandedly, on the other hand, "is never used in this way . . . It almost always means 'casually.'" And it has won over even John Simon, the arts critic and language stickler, who's quoted in *MWDEU* describing something as "imperturbably snobbish and offhandedly puncturing." See *Secondhand, Underhand.*

On the Street. A street comprises the roadway and the buildings at each side. Say, in the street. He lives in Broadway.

· · ·

On the street where you live, or *in* the street? Americans hadn't yet made a final choice, and the 19th-century commentators tended to prefer the British usage. Some tried applying logic: White 1870 argued that *in* was the preposition to use for a limited surface like a street, while *on* belonged to surfaces "without visible boundaries," such as fields. Baker 1907 voted for *on*: "Inasmuch as the street includes the sidewalks and the road-bed, one does not live in the street unless one is homeless or friendless." Ransom 1911 agreed, and tried to counter White's logic with his own: "The use of 'in the street' for 'on the street' dates back to the days when people almost literally lived 'in the street.' Then the streets were so narrow that 'in' was proper."

We don't really know why Americans have chosen to live *on* Elm Street and Britons *in* Elm Street, but we can guess that logic has very little to do with it.

One Another for **Each Other**. See *Each Other*.

Only. "He only had one." Say, He had only one, or, better, one only. The other sentence might be taken to mean that only he had one; that, indeed, is what it distinctly says. The correct placing of only in a sentence requires attention and skill.

· · ·

Robert Lowth was probably the first to point out that "I only spake three words" and "I spake only three words" differed in "propriety and force," though he did not claim, as later critics did, that they actually had different meanings. In his own writing, Lowth generally placed *only* as close as possible to the element it modified. But not always: Early in the pages of his *English Grammar* (1763) we find, "He only meant to acknowledge [Jesus] to be an extraordinary person." Later in the book comes "*Let* does not only express permission; but praying, exhorting, commanding."

Bierce, and many later editors, would insist on relocating those *only*s. But would it make a difference? Usage writers love to ring the changes on *only*, comparing "*Only* I want a cup of tea," "I *only* want a cup of tea," "I want *only* a cup of tea," and so on. In the wild, however, *only* is almost never truly ambiguous. And too-strict observance of the rule creates an unnatural, overemphatic construction: "I want only a drink of water." In some cases, too, *only* modifies a phrase or an entire sentence, and shouldn't be moved: "We were only trying to help."

Fowler 1926 blamed the *only* fetish on pedants who wanted to make English "an exact science or an automatic machine." Yet in 2009, syndicated language maven James J. Kilpatrick was still writing an annual column on the importance of *only*. All this is a waste of time, as Fowler said it would be. We use *only* pretty much as Lowth used it two and a half centuries ago, and as we would probably be using it if he and his acolytes had never written a word on the subject.

Opine for **Think**. The word is not very respectably connected.

• • •

Opine's relations are as respectable as Bierce's—it was adopted from French in the 15th century. But despite its usefulness to journalists, it has never been entirely domesticated. Bain 1863 thought it was still "not fully adopted into the language," and Webster 1913 labeled it a Southern usage. It's still not taken quite seriously, says *MWDEU*; it shows "an undeniable tendency to turn up in humorous writing." Even Bierce could see the aptness of *opine* for light verse like "The Fall of Miss Larkin":

> *This I know from testimony, though a critic, I opine,*
> *Needs an ear that is in some respects dissimilar to mine.*
> *She could sing, too, like a jaybird, and they say*
>   *all eyes were wet*
> *When Sally and the ranch-dog were performing a duet . . .*

Opposite for **Contrary**. "I hold the opposite opinion." "The opposite practice."

• • •

Trench 1852 was not the earliest commentator to articulate Bierce's distinction, but he was among the most lucid: "'Opposites' *complete,* while 'contraries' *exclude* one another . . . For example, a man may be at once prudent and bold, for these are opposites; he could not be at once prudent and rash, for these are contraries." Everyday English doesn't, and probably never did, make much use of these fine distinctions. Bernstein 1965 reviewed the difference between *contrary* and *opposite* (and *converse* and *reverse*), but he sensibly recommended using *reverse,* the most general term, "unless the writer has a special purpose in mind."

Or for Nor. Probably our most nearly universal solecism. "I cannot see the sun or the moon." This means that I am unable to see one of them, though I may see the other. By using nor, I affirm the invisibility of both, which is what I wanted to do. If a man is not white or black he may nevertheless be a Negro or a Caucasian; but if he is not white nor black he belongs to some other race. See *Neither.*

. . .

Bierce's interpretation of the impact of *or* for *nor* is so outlandish it's hard to grasp—or believe. But yes, he really is saying that "I can't see the sun *or* the moon" means, "Either I can't see the sun or I can't see the moon, but I do see one of them."

It's safe to say no reader or listener from King Alfred to the present would take the sentence that way. Bierce's fellow usage critics habitually used *or* in such negative constructions, apparently with no fear of misleading readers: "It sometimes happens also, that the word . . . *does not sound easily or agreeably*" (Lowth 1763).* "*Monetary*: A word of recent origin, *not in Johnson or Todd*" (Bartlett 1848) (emphasis added).

Bierce seems to have picked up the *neither* . . . *nor* rule and run

* Today we would say the word "does not sound *easy* or agreeable." But the usage fraternity had not yet agreed on whether the adverb or adjective was more correct with a linking verb.

off a cliff with it, failing to notice that his "universal solecism," properly translated, means "standard English usage."

Ordinarily for **Usually.** Clumsy.

• • •

Usually is the senior synonym, it's true, by a century or so. But *ordinarily* dates to 1555, so you'd have to call it mature by 1909. Bierce's fellow usage writers apparently did not agree that *ordinarily* was "clumsy," for they used it as anyone else would, as an alternative to *usually, generally, normally,* or *commonly.*

Outside of. Omit the preposition.

• • •

Language tidiers of the "omit needless words" persuasion all think *outside of* is bad.* Robert Palfrey Utter, for instance, in *Every-Day Words and Their Uses* (1916): "*Of* is incorrect after the preposition *outside.*"

Real people use *outside of* whenever it sounds natural. Robert Palfrey Utter, for instance, in the same book: "Local, provincial, and dialect words are those which† do not pass current outside of certain regions," he wrote. And "as applied to persons . . . [*raise*] is now little used outside of the United States." And *donate* is "little used outside of the United States." Writers may do as he says, or do as he did.

Ovation. In ancient Rome an ovation was an inferior triumph accorded to victors in minor wars or unimportant battle. Its

---

* The *outside of* that means "except for"—as in Groucho Marx's "Outside of a dog, a book is man's best friend. Inside of a dog, it's too dark to read"—is a different animal; it always takes the *of.*

† In 1916, the *which-that* rule had not yet reached critical mass among usage mavens; educated writers were still free to use *which* in restrictive clauses, as Utter does here, without fear of finger-wagging *which*-hunters. See *That.*

character and limitations, like those of the triumph, were strictly defined by law and custom. An enthusiastic demonstration in honor of an American civilian is nothing like that, and should not be called by its name.

. . .

Bryant 1870 put *ovation* on his list of words banned at the *New York Evening Post*—no reason given—and that was enough to spook American journalists for decades. "Most good newspapers consider [*ovation*] extravagant, and some bar it altogether," said Ransom 1911. "The word should be reserved for a really great occasion." But the French and Italians had already adapted their versions of *ovation* for use in the sense "applause"; speakers of English, seeing no particular need for the old Roman sense of the word, ignored the classicists and followed suit.

Over for **About, In,** or **Concerning.** "Don't cry over spilt milk." "He rejoiced over his acquittal."

. . .

Over had been used in this way since Old English, but what was good enough for King Alfred, William Caxton, Shakespeare, and Hardy was apparently too imprecise for Ambrose G. Bierce.

Over for **More than.** "A sum of over ten thousand dollars." "Upward of ten thousand dollars" is equally objectionable.

. . .

One day in the mid-19th century, William Cullen Bryant decided that *over* should not be used to mean "more than." His 1870 *Index Expurgatorius* outlawed expressions like "over $60" and "over seven miles" at the newspaper he edited, and his rule soon spread throughout America's newsrooms.

We don't know if Bryant actually invented the "rule" or found it in an unknown source, but it's as mythical as the unicorn. *Over* has meant "more than" for a thousand years; the usage has never been wrong, except in the glazed eyes of editors and English teachers who drank the Kool-Aid Bryant and Bierce were serving. It may be that only the death of the newspaper will kill off this parasitic superstition; dictionaries and common sense have so far had no effect.

Over for **On**. "The policeman struck him over the head." If the blow was over the head it did not hit him.

· · ·

"Over the head" is perfectly ordinary English, in use at least two and a half centuries before Bierce noticed it. But there must have been other dogged literalists who read it Bierce's way. As late as 1964, Roy Copperud felt the need to defend it: "Some harbor the delusion that it is wrong to say a man was hit over the head, unless the blows missed him," he noted in *A Dictionary of Usage and Style*. "This is a standard sense of the word ('down upon from above'), however, and instantly clear except to those who willfully misunderstand."

Over with. "Let us have it over with." Omit with. A better expression is, Let us get done with it.

· · ·

The *OED*'s earliest example of this usage, from 1822, is a longer form that Bierce might have liked better: "It will be hard work to get through the three months to Cousin Maria's wedding; I wish it were 'over and done with.'" These days we "get it over with," and though the idiom is informal, nobody is trying to ban it from English.

P

Pair for **Pairs**. If a word has a good plural use each form in its place.

. . .

That is, don't say "two pair of trousers" (or, especially, "two pair of pants"—see *Pants*). The logical Bierce wanted everyone to say "one pair, two pairs." But the consensus was against him: "This word remains *pair* in the plural when it is preceded by a number," said Frank Vizetelly in *A Desk-Book of Errors* (1906): "Two *pair* of gloves," but "many *pairs* of trousers." Since the mid-20th century, usagists have been promoting the "good plural" form Bierce favored—"two pairs"—and it is now the favored usage. But "two pair" is still standard English.

Pants for **Trousers**. Abbreviated from pantaloons, which are no longer worn. Vulgar exceedingly.

. . .

"Vulgar exceedingly"? Strong words, but Bierce was not the only critic who found *pants* repellent. Oliver Wendell Holmes had declared back in 1846 that *pants* was "a word not made for gentlemen, but 'gents.'"

One strike against *pants* was the company it kept; the dudes and dandies of the 1840s, in their stylish tight trousers with straps under the instep, had adopted the word. Edgar Allan Poe had a character bill his tailor for promotional duties: "Standing on one leg three hours, to show off new-style strapped pants at 12½ cents per leg per hour, 37½."

Another problem was the British sense of *pants*. While American men called their underwear "drawers," for Englishmen those garments were (and still are) "pants." Bierce spent three years in

England during the 1870s, so he would have been aware of the difference. And Bierce was known for his modesty; he told friends that no woman, including his wife, had ever seen him naked. Mercifully, he lived in the time of Queen Victoria, not Victoria's Secret. See *Gents*.

Partially for **Partly**. A dictionary word, to swell the book.

• • •

In *The Devil's Dictionary*, Bierce called the lexicographer "a pestilent fellow" whose whims loused up the language. But *partially* can't be called dictionary padding; it had earned its spot by working hard since 1475, half a century before *partly* arrived in English.

The words coexisted peacefully until 1870, when William Cullen Bryant banned the use of *partially* at his newspaper and Richard Grant White argued that it should mean only "in a partial or biased way," a sense then dying out. The debate would simmer for decades; in *Modern English Usage* (1926), H. W. Fowler complicated it further by suggesting that *partly* should mean "as regards a part" ("partly due to cowardice") and *partially* only "to a limited degree" ("a partially drunken sailor"). But even Fowler had to admit that the words were often interchangeable, and so they remain today.

Party for **Person**. "A party named Brown." The word, used in that sense, has the excuse that it is a word. Otherwise it is no better than "pants" and "gent." A person making an agreement, however, is a party to that agreement.

• • •

Party for *person*, though used in English since the 15th century, had been borrowed from the legal lexicon and repurposed as a journalistic affectation. The *OED*, in 1905, called it "formerly common and in serious use; now shoppy, vulgar, or jocular." Bierce doesn't mention that "jocular" usage, but he knew it and used it: "The old gray-headed party who lost his life last Friday at the jeweled hands of our wife deserves more than a passing notice," he wrote in one of his newspaper columns.

Patron for Customer.

• • •

Merchants in the 19th century had begun to call their customers "patrons," and several critics thought the word once used for sponsors of Michelangelo and Mozart was too classy for such commercial use. "'Patrons' should not be used for 'customers,'" said Vizetelly 1906. "A *patron* is one who fosters a person or thing; a *customer* is one who deals regularly at one establishment." Fifty years later, Partridge was still insisting that one could be a "'patron of the arts,' but not of a greengrocer or a bookmaker. Tradesmen have *customers,* professional men have *clients*." Their campaign may have had some effect; today, says *MWDEU, patrons* is more commonly used for "customers of restaurants, bars, hotels, theaters, and the like" than for retail shoppers.

Pay for Give, Make, etc. "He pays attention." "She paid a visit to Niagara." It is conceivable that one may owe attention or a visit to another person, but one cannot be indebted to a place.

• • •

Bierce's anti-commercial antennae are oversensitive, leading him to read "pay attention" as a vulgar monetary metaphor. In fact, "pay attention" and "pay a visit" were current by the 17th century, and even then "pay a visit" had only the faintest aura of obligation. Bierce seems to be alone in this animus; his fellow critic Alfred Ayres, in *The Verbalist* (1881), used the expression himself, writing of "those who pay attention" to punctuation.

Pay. "Laziness does not pay." "It does not pay to be uncivil." This use of the word is grossly commercial. Say, Indolence is unprofitable. There is no advantage in incivility.

· · ·

How is it that Bierce sees a commercial taint in "laziness does not pay," but not in "indolence is unprofitable"? In any case, his denunciation was out of date. The figurative use of *to pay*, implying a nonmonetary reward, appears in a 1658 example in the *OED*: "Serve honesty ever . . . she will pay, if slow."

Peculiar for **Odd**, or **Unusual.** Also sometimes used to denote distinction, or particularity. Properly a thing is peculiar only to another thing, of which it is characteristic, nothing else having it; as knowledge of the use of fire is peculiar to Man.

· · ·

Bierce is fighting a rearguard action here, and a misguided one as well. The original sense of *peculiar* was "distinct," the sense he seems to just tolerate; his favored meaning, "characteristic," came later. And the sense he disparages—"odd, unusual"—had been current since the 1700s. Bierce's preferred *peculiar* is still in use, in constructions like "characteristics peculiar to each species." But the "odd" sense of *peculiar* is strong enough that some people would use "particular to each species," to avoid confusion. And few nowadays would venture to say, for instance, "every writer has a peculiar style."

Peek for **Peep.** Seldom heard in England, though common here. "I peeked out through the curtain and saw him." That it is a variant of peep is seen in the child's word peek-a-boo, equivalent to bo-peep. Better use the senior word.

· · ·

Most other critics ignored *peek*, but Seth T. Hurd, in *A Grammatical Corrector* (1847), quoted an unspecified edition of Webster's *Dictionary* that calls it "a New England perversion." Bierce and

Webster were wrong, however, about *peep*'s seniority. *Peek* appeared in Chaucer, before 1400; *peep* ambled along, dragging her tail behind her, roughly a century later. The British still say *peep-bo*, and Americans *peek-a-boo*, but since the origin of the words is unknown, neither can claim etymological superiority. Both *peek* and *peep* are standard.

People for **Persons**. "Three people were killed." "Many people are superstitious." People has retained its parity of meaning with the Latin populus, whence it comes, and the word is not properly used except to designate a population, or large fractions of it considered in the mass. To speak of any stated or small number of persons as people is incorrect.

. . .

A few 19th-century writers had mentioned the issue, but the *people*-vs.-*persons* debate didn't really take off till the dawn of the 20th century. There were several twists to the anti-*people* rule. Some critics didn't like "several people" and "many people"; others, like Bierce, thought you shouldn't use numbers, at least small numbers, with *people*. "It is always incorrect to use people in speaking of a few persons; as, 'There were only three people present,'" instructed *Correct English* magazine in 1901. It's true that Chaucer, in *The Knight's Tale* (1385), had described "the palace full of people, up and down, here three, there ten"—but he didn't know any better.

William Strunk Jr., in the 1918 version of *Elements of Style*, repeated a zinger* to prove that *people* couldn't be the plural

---

* Ben Zimmer, executive producer of the *Visual Thesaurus* Web site, traced Strunk's example to a letter in the January 16, 1897, issue of the New York literary journal *The Critic*: "There is one word which is misused by every journalist and every author wherever the English language is written—the word 'people.' Mr. Howells, for instance, in one of his delightful novels speaks of 'three people' sitting in a room. Now, if two of these 'people' were to withdraw, one 'people' would be left—and very much left! It seems unnecessary to state—and yet it is necessary to state it—that 'people' is a collective noun."

of *persons*: "If of 'six people' five went away, how many 'people' would be left?" (A version of this witless riddle is preserved, like a fossilized cockroach, in the 1999 fourth edition of *Elements of Style*.) Except for browbeaten journalists, however, native speakers of English do not say "five persons were on the doorstep."

Per. "Five dollars per day." "Three per hundred." Say, three dollars a day; three in a hundred. If you must use the Latin preposition use the Latin noun too: per diem; per centum.

· · ·

The idea that *per* was a foreign word, appropriate only with other Latin words, was a late-19th-century notion. "*Per* is correct before Latin nouns only; as, per annum, per diem, per cent., etc.," said Ayres 1881. But Theodore Bernstein, in *The Careful Writer* (1965), showed that such foolish consistency can make for strange sentences: "The Soviet shoe industry produced about three shoes for each person." Whether the noun is English or Latin, said Bernstein, "*per* meaning 'for each' is natural and desirable in any statistical or economic context." Even Bierce agreed, at least unconsciously: "I was to do one article per issue," he wrote to his boss, William Randolph Hearst, in 1909.

Perpetually for **Continually**. "The child is perpetually asking questions." What is done perpetually is done continually and forever.

· · ·

Perpetually does literally mean "eternally," but Bierce's example sounds more like hyperbole than a mistake. In fact, *A Dictionary of Contemporary American Usage* (1957) specifically mentions a similar, semi-jocular use: *Perpetually*, it notes, "is also, in the exaggeration with which irritation relieves itself, used for *continually*, especially in expression of minor annoyance (*The children are perpetually demanding to go to the zoo*)." Perhaps this *perpetually* was an irritating usage tic in earlier decades, but it no longer plagues us.

Phenomenal for **Extraordinary**, or **Surprising**. Everything that occurs is phenomenal, for all that we know about is phenomena, appearances. Of realities, noumena, we are ignorant.

. . .

Bierce would like the philosophical sense to be the only sense of *phenomenon*, but it was too late. The word had been used to mean "an amazing person" as early as 1730, when Pope wrote in a letter, "Have you seen or convers'd with Mr. Chubb, who is a wonderful Phenomenon of Wiltshire?" *Phenomenal* for "extraordinary" came later—it was new in the mid-19th century—and Bierce's usage contemporaries found it excessive, slangy, and, of course, vulgar. Partridge carried on, insisting into the mid-20th century, in *Usage and Abusage*, that "phenomenal should not be debased to equivalence with unusual"; the users of *phenomenal* ignored the scolds, as slang users always do.

Plead (pronounced "pled") for **Pleaded**. "He plead guilty."

. . .

The irregular past tense *pled* was much newer than *pleaded*, but it was popular in America, where it was often spelled *plead*. "In nine cases out of ten, where the verb to plead is used in the past tense, it is spoken and written as if its conjugation were analogous to *read*," complained Edward S. Gould in *Good English* (1867). "But that is not the formation of the verb. It is analogous to *knead*, *kneaded*; and is *plead*, *pleaded*." Most authorities today prefer *pleaded*, but *pled*—which has shed its alternative *plead* spelling—has its fans, especially in legal circles. Both forms are standard American.

Plenty for **Plentiful**. "Fish and fowl were plenty."

. . .

Samuel Johnson called this *plenty* a barbarism, though he noted that Shakespeare had used it (in *II Henry IV*): "If reasons were as plenty as blackberries, I would give no man a reason upon compulsion." The usage dated to the 14th century, but by Bierce's time it was considered either old-fashioned or inelegant, and it soon ceased to trouble the critics.

Poetess. A foolish word, like "authoress."

. . .

Here Bierce echoes Edward S. Gould, whose analysis in *Good English* (1867) struck a faintly feminist note: Such gendered nouns were "philological absurdities, because they are fabricated on the false assumption that their primaries [or source words] indicate *men*." But in fact, said Gould, a conductor "is a *person* who conducts; director, a person who directs; inspector, a person who inspects; waiter, a person who waits." Besides, he said, if *poetess* and *conductress* are allowed, what's to stop horrors like *writeress, officeress, manageress, superintendentess*, and *talkeress*? See *Authoress*.

Poetry for **Verse**. Not all verse is poetry; not all poetry is verse. Few persons can know, or hope to know, the one from the other, but he who has the humility to doubt (if such a one there be) should say verse if the composition is metrical.

. . .

Bierce would have liked to be a great poet, but he called himself a versifier, and he thought others should be equally modest. "To verse-makers, as verse-makers, I have no objection," he wrote in 1877. "It is only when the verse-maker fancies himself a poetry-maker that he becomes offensive . . . It is important that the broad and sharp distinction between verse and poetry be as clearly perceived and sacredly respected by my brother rhymesters as it is by myself."

A sample of Bierce's verse, from the entry on Brahma in *The Devil's Dictionary*:

> O Brahma, thou rare old Divinity,
> First Person of the Hindoo Trinity,
> You sit there so calm and securely,
> With feet folded up so demurely—
> You're the First Person Singular, surely.

Point Blank. "He fired at him point blank." This usually is intended to mean directly, or at short range. But point blank means the point at which the line of sight is crossed downward by the trajectory—the curve described by the missile.

· · ·

Bierce's technical definition of *point blank* is a minority one, labeled "obsolete" and "rare" in the *OED*. Both of the dictionary's citations for this sense come from 19th-century military manuals, though, and Bierce, having served in the Civil War, may have prided himself on that specialized knowledge. The senses Bierce rejects, however—"with horizontal aim" or "so close that the shooter can aim straight at the target, without allowing for the fall of the projectile"—had been in use since the 16th century; they were the common meanings of *point blank* in his day, as they are in ours.

Poisonous for **Venomous**. Hemlock is poisonous, but a rattlesnake is venomous.

· · ·

As usual, Bierce would like to fence the overlapping words into separate pens. But while *venomous* does describe rattlesnakes and other animals that poison victims with a bite or sting, *poisonous* has always been a broader term. Samuel Johnson knew both

words, but in his *Dictionary* (1755) he referred to "a poisonous ser-
pent," "a poisonous insect," and "a poisonous reptile."

Paul Brians's Web site, *Common Errors in English*, is among the
contemporary sources that support Bierce's distinction. "A snake
or tarantula is not itself poisonous because if you eat one it won't
poison you," writes Brians. "A blowfish will kill you if you eat it,
so it is poisonous; but it is not venomous." That's good to know,
but in nonspecialist contexts, it's still permissible to call a rattlesnake poisonous.

Politics. The word is not plural because it happens to end with s.

• • •

True enough: *Politics* is plural, but not because it ends with *s*; it's
plural because writers and speakers have been construing it as
plural for centuries. Swift, that would-be reformer of the English
language, used it as a plural in 1706: "Politics . . . are nothing but
corruptions, and are consequently of no use to a good king."

The singular *politics* emerged only in the 18th century, and it remained a minority usage in Bierce's time. In his 1917 book *English
Usage*, J. Lesslie Hall tallied examples from well-known writers.
"The word *politics* is plural by a ratio of 30 to 9 authorities, 52 to
10 passages," Hall reported. "These facts refute the opinions of
some . . . grammarians and rhetorical scholars . . . Polite colloquial
usage is probably in favor of the plural." Today's usage is in favor
of the singular, but *politics* still works both ways.

**Possess for Have. "To possess knowledge is to possess power."
Possess is lacking in naturalness and unduly emphasizes the
concept of ownership.**

• • •

Possess is no doubt a bit formal, compared to *have*, but "unduly
emphasizes the concept of ownership" is a stretch. In practice,
Bierce used the word himself, as anyone might, when formality

seemed appropriate; in the essay "Civilization," for instance, he wrote, "It is a universal human weakness to disparage the knowledge that we do not ourselves possess."

Practically for **Virtually**. This error is very common. "It is practically conceded." "The decision was practically unanimous." "The panther and the cougar are practically the same animal." These and similar misapplications of the word are virtually without excuse.

. . .

Practically had been used for "virtually" for more than a century before Bierce wrote, and he was apparently the first to call this extension of sense an error, though not the last. By 1965, however, *practically* and *virtually* were "just about interchangeable," said Theodore Bernstein. "Half a century from now they most likely will be completely so." His forecast came true ahead of schedule, as *AHD4* explained in a Usage Note: "Language critics sometimes object when the notion of practicality is stripped from this word in its further extension to mean 'all but, nearly,' as in *He had practically finished his meal when I arrived.* But this usage is widely used by reputable writers and must be considered acceptable."

Predicate for **Found**, or **Base**. "I predicate my argument on universal experience." What is predicated of something is affirmed as an attribute of it, as omnipotence is predicated of the Deity.

. . .

The use of *predicate* for "base" is an American innovation dating from the mid-18th century, says the *OED*. George Washington used it: "Was not the first application to you predicated on this information?" But on its way to standard status, it had to fight a phalanx of 19th-century usage writers.

Gould 1867 was especially scathing: "Ignorant usage—and very ignorant usage it must be—in the United States, has recently paraded predicate in the sense of *to found*; as, 'his argument was *predicated* on the assumption' . . . The word is used in that sense in the pulpit, at the bar, and *of course* in novels and newspapers . . . Yet, mad as the people may be on this point, it seems that one lexicographer is 'as mad as they.' The last Revised Edition of Webster gives as a secondary definition of predicate, 'To rest upon for proof, or as an assertion or an opinion; to found; to base.'"

Eventually, of course, the mad people and their equally mad lexicographers got their way. Today, even in Britain, *predicated* can mean "based on," if that's what we need it to mean.

Prejudice for **Prepossession.** Literally, a prejudice is merely a prejudgment—a decision before evidence—and may be favorable or unfavorable, but it is so much more frequently used in the latter sense than in the former that clarity is better got by the other word for reasonless approval.

. . .

Both *prejudice* and *prepossession* started out meaning merely "prejudgment," but they diverged, over the years, to mean (mostly) "bias against" and "bias in favor of," respectively. As early as 1818, George Crabb, in *English Synonymes*, said that *prejudice* was usually negative. In 1881, Alfred Ayres went further: "We sometimes hear the expression, 'He is prejudiced in his favor,' but this can not be accounted a good use of the word," he wrote in *The Verbalist*. Ayres would be surprised to find that today *prepossessed* is fairly rare; despite the waste of words, many people prefer to write "prejudiced in favor."

Preparedness for **Readiness.** An awkward and needless word much used in discussion of national armaments, as, "Our preparedness for war."

. . .

Yes, *preparedness* is clunky, and Bierce seems to think it's a journalistic vogue word. But it's not (or not only) a fad; it goes back to the 16th century. Bierce was apparently alone in opposing it; Ayres 1881, writing on a different topic, commented that "*obligingness, preparedness,* and *designedly* seem quite natural." *Preparedness* is hardly a casual word—it is still most at home in discussions of national armaments—but it is a word in good standing.

Preside. "Professor Swackenhauer presided at the piano." "The deviled crab table was presided over by Mrs. Dooley." How would this sound? "The ginger pop stand was under the administration of President Woolwit, and Professor Sooffle presided at the flute."

. . .

"How would this sound?" asks Bierce. It would sound like an item in the social pages of a local newspaper, that's how. And *preside* took a predictable route to that slightly undignified spot. As early as the 17th century, it meant "sit at the head of the table"; in the 18th century, a hostess would "preside" at the tea table, except at a large party, when her friends took over the honored role. The social *preside* was so unremarkable that usagist William Mathews, in a chapter of his book devoted to grandiose language, used the verb quite unselfconsciously: "[He] found no one at home except his niece, who presided at the tea table" (*Words; Their Use and Abuse,* 1876).

To extend *preside* from the tea table to the ginger pop stand may well be a step too far; but then, it's not easy to report on the management of the ginger pop stand without sounding ridiculous, whatever verb the reporter uses.

Pretend for Profess. "I do not pretend to be infallible." Of course not; one does not care to confess oneself a pretender. To pretend is to try to deceive; one may profess quite honestly.

. . .

Pretend certainly can mean "try to deceive," but the sense Bierce rejects—"claim," as in "I don't pretend to have the answer"—had been popular for centuries before he decided it must be wrong. Johnson's *Dictionary* (1755) included the definition "To put in a claim truly or falsely; . . . to profess presumptuously." Bierce appears once again to be indulging his mania for neatness, and pretending that a word doesn't mean what it clearly does mean.

Preventative for **Preventive**. No such word as preventative.

• • •

There was and is such a word as *preventative*, of course; it arrived in English only a few decades after *preventive*, in the mid-17th century. Two hundred years later, Hurd 1847 decided the longer spelling was "a common error"; it took another couple of decades for usage critics to declare it nonexistent. *Preventative* is longer and less common than *preventive*, and no doubt is a "needless variant," but its enemies have not yet managed to drive it out of use, or out of our dictionaries.

Previous for **Previously**. "The man died previous to receipt of the letter."

• • •

Previous to is a compound preposition, says *MWDEU*, that was first recorded in the 17th century, then attacked in the late 18th as "not good English." Later authorities have been all over the map: Fowler, the Evanses, and Bernstein had no problem with *previous to*; Partridge called it "commercialese"; Garner says it's "highfalutin." *Previous to* is less common than it used to be, but not because we've taken Bierce's advice to make it *previously to*. Most of us just say *before*.

Prior to for **Before**. Stilted.

• • •

Bierce was an early opponent of *prior to*; before the 20th century, most usagists not only did not disparage the phrase but used it themselves. Critics since Bierce, however, have attacked it on various grounds: it's stuffy, it's bureaucratic, it's faddish. Theodore Bernstein, in *The Careful Writer* (1965), demanded, "Would you say *posterior to* in place of *after*?" *Prior to* is still used, of course, though *MWDEU* notes that it mainly appears in "formal or impersonal" contexts—just the contexts in which those 19th-century language mavens used it so freely.

Proportions for **Dimensions**. "A rock of vast proportions." Proportions relate to form; dimensions to magnitude.

• • •

A century and more before Bierce's dictum, *proportions* was used loosely to mean merely size. Gothic novelist Ann Radcliffe, in *The Italian* (1797), described "cliffs of naked marble of such gigantic proportions, that they were awful even at a distance."

The objection to such use seems to have been new when Bierce was compiling his blacklist. Scott and Denney 1900 gave the example "The doctor wore an old white hat of enormous proportions," along with a warning: "This use of proportions is not recognized by any good authority." Not in 1900, perhaps, but Webster 1828 had listed "form, size" as a little-used sense of *proportions*. And though some critics have labeled it informal, this sense of the word has remained standard.

Propose for **Purpose**, or **Intend**. "I propose to go to Europe." A mere intention is not a proposal.

• • •

Purpose and *propose* are actually variants of the same word, and the *OED* shows that *propose* was used to mean "intend" as early as Chaucer, circa 1390. The earliest objection I find is in George Crabb's *English Synonymes* (1818); Crabb, like Bierce, seems to think *propose* is the more serious word, *purpose* the expression of a passing whim. "We PURPOSE . . . that which is near at hand, or immediately to be set about; we PROPOSE that which is more distant: the former requires the setting before one's mind, the latter requires deliberation."

Many usage writers since Bierce have urged separating the words in some way: *"To purpose* is to have an intention to do something, *to propose* is to declare this intention," suggested Scott and Denney 1900. But most people have found it simpler just to abandon the verb *purpose*.

Proposition for **Proposal**. "He made a proposition." In current slang almost anything is a proposition. A difficult enterprise is "a tough proposition," an agile wrestler, "a slippery proposition," and so forth.

. . .

Bierce is combining two usage criticisms here. *Proposition* meaning "proposal" was well established, dating to the 14th century, and had only recently attracted some mild criticism. Ayres 1881, for instance, thought *proposal* might be better because it "has but one meaning, and is shorter by one syllable." Bierce probably wasn't interested in that fine distinction, though. The recent slang use—"tough proposition" and the like—was more likely the red flag that got him pawing and snorting.

Proven for **Proved**. Good Scotch, but bad English.

. . .

Proven, though it was four hundred years old when Bierce opined on it, was widely considered a Scottish barbarism or even a vulgarism. But if it was bad English, it proved to be good American: By the mid-20th century it was used more often than *proved* in the

United States, according to Evans and Evans 1957. And the usage wave has now rebounded eastward: According to the *OED*'s 2008 data, *proven* is not only the usual North American adjective, "it is now also more frequent than PROVED . . . in British English."

Proverbial for **Familiar.** "The proverbial dog in the manger." The animal is not "proverbial" for it is not mentioned in a proverb, but in a fable.

. . .

So, we should refer to "the fabulous dog in the manger"? That doesn't sound right. And in fact, *proverbial* was never limited to the literal sense "found in a proverb"; from the time the adjective appeared, in the 15th century, it was used to mean "resembling, characteristic of, or of the nature of a proverb," in the words of the *OED*. Webster 1828 concurred: *Proverbial* meant "resembling a proverb, suitable to a proverb," whether or not a proverb was involved. Opposition to the proverb-free *proverbial* still haunts American newsrooms, but not their official stylebooks; Bierce may have been the only critic literal-minded enough to put this peeve on the record.

Q

Quit for **Cease, Stop.** "Jones promises to quit drinking." In another sense, too, the word is commonly misused, as, "He has quit the town." Say, quitted.

. . .

In 17th-century England, you could "quit a job" or "quit whoring," but two hundred years later only Americans were still using the verb to mean "discontinue." Apparently that was enough to ruin its reputation. Asked why this "generally recognized usage" was condemned, Utter 1916 just sputtered: "The answer is that it is generally recognized as vulgar."

In the sense "leave, depart," *quit* was still acceptable everywhere. Bierce's only problem with it is the irregular past tense, *quit*, which he wants to restore to the traditional *quitted*. See *Bet, Wed*.

Quite. "She is quite charming." If it is meant that she is entirely charming this is right, but usually the meaning intended to be conveyed is less than that—that she is rather, or somewhat, charming.

• • •

Quite meaning "rather, very" was already three hundred years old when Bierce groused about it. True, its other sense—"completely, entirely"—was even older, but most of the usage critics had managed to wrap their minds around both senses.

R

Raise for **Bring up, Grow, Breed,** etc. In this country a word-of-all-work: "raise children," "raise wheat," "raise cattle." Children are brought up, grain, hay and vegetables are grown, animals and poultry are bred.

• • •

Americans have been anxious about "raising" children for about two hundred years, ever since the idiom fell out of use in Britain. Plagued by a linguistic inferiority complex, says *MWDEU*, American critics began disparaging *raise* as provincial or Southern or just plain wrong. Frank Vizetelly, in *A Desk-Book of Errors* (1906), told people they should *rear* cattle, *raise* chickens, and *bring up* children. Those people were too busy raising their cattle, chickens, and children to pay the slightest attention, and after several more decades of frustration, the usage mavens finally gave up.

Real for **Really**, or **Very**. "It is real good of him." "The weather was real cold."

. . .

No doubt Bierce believed, as most people do, that *real* was just a casual short form of *really*, but the story is more complicated. This *real* once had a separate existence as an adjective in northern English and Scottish dialects; a 1658 citation in the *OED* has "the reallest good turn that can be done." Though it later came to look like an adverb, *real* is really an intensifier, not a full-service adverb, and is often used in expressions where *really* would not fit. *Real* is equivalent to *very*, and is used only to modify adjectives and adverbs, notes *MWDEU*, while *really* more often means *truly*, and not just *very*.

As Evans and Evans 1957 summed it up: "This use of *real* is accepted spoken English in most parts of the United States but does not appear in formal, or impersonal, writing. The adverb *really* does not have this meaning. *I will write really soon* is neither natural nor literary English."

Realize for **Conceive**, or **Comprehend**. "I could not realize the situation." Writers caring for precision use this word in the sense of to make real, not to make seem real. A dream seems real, but is actually realized when made to come true.

. . .

"His ambition was realized when he got a recording contract"— that would be the only proper use of the verb for Bierce. But both branches of meaning—"make real" and "make to seem real," or "bring vividly to mind"—are legitimate, dating to the 17th century. Today's dominant sense of *realize*—"to fully grasp, understand"— is an 18th-century development, according to the *OED*, and mostly North American. That history may account for Bierce's prejudice against the usage, but only because he was a stubborn traditionalist;

Webster 1828 had accepted the disputed sense well before Bierce was born.

Recollect for **Remember**. To remember is to have in memory; to recollect is to recall what has escaped from memory. We remember automatically; in recollecting we make a conscious effort.

. . .

Maybe if you were trained from toddlerhood, you could see a difference between *remember* and *recollect*. Or maybe not. But this was a popular peeve among 19th-century usage writers. "When we don't remember what we wish to speak of, we try to re-collect it," said White 1870.

It's not as simple as it sounds. Wouldn't this distinction mean it was always wrong to say "I can't remember," since if you're *trying* to remember, the verb should be *recollect*? And even if the writer uses *remember* and *recollect* differently, will the reader notice? How would you tell?

Garner 2003 and *MWDEU* mention the distinction, but they don't clear up the mystery. The only usage difference I'm certain of is one also noted in *MWDEU*: "For many writers the real distinguishing characteristic of *recollect* seems to be that it has a folksy quality."

Redeem for **Retrieve**. "He redeemed his good name." Redemption (Latin redemptio, from re and dimere) is allied to ransom, and carries the sense of buying back; whereas to retrieve is merely to recover what was lost.

. . .

The idea that redemption involves a literal ransom may be Bierce's own etymological fantasy. Whatever its source, it doesn't jibe with the history of the (nontheological) *redeem*. Crabb 1818 called the verb "a term of general application . . . we may *redeem* our character, *redeem* our life, or *redeem* our honor." He quoted a verse from John Gay's *Fables* (1727): "So live in credit and esteem, And the good name you lost, redeem."

For Bierce, *redeem* may stink of commerce—pawnshops, even!—but Bierce's nose sometimes led him astray. When people redeem their reputations, cash is not (necessarily) part of the transaction.

Redound for Conduce. "A man's honesty redounds to his advantage." We make a better use of the word if we say of one (for example) who has squandered a fortune, that its loss redounds to his advantage, for the word denotes a fluctuation, as from seeming evil to actual good; as villification may direct attention to one's excellent character.

· · ·

Redound, literally "surge back," has a lot of legitimate uses, and only Bierce seems to think it should connote a surprising reversal. Webster 1828, for instance, gives *conduce* and *result* as synonyms for *redound*, with the example "The honor done to our religion ultimately redounds to God."

Refused. "He was refused a crown." It is the crown that was refused to him. See *Given*.

Regular for Natural, or Customary. "Flattery of the people is the demagogue's regular means to political preferment." Regular properly relates to a rule (regula) more definite than the law of antecedent and consequent.

· · ·

Maybe this *regular* sounded overly casual to Bierce. But the "habitual, constant" sense of *regular* dates to 1797, and nobody else in the usage game heard anything odd in it.

Reliable for **Trusty**, or **Trustworthy**. A word not yet admitted to the vocabulary of the fastidious, but with a strong backing for the place.

• • •

Reliable was coined in the 16th century, but it lay low till the mid-19th, when it suddenly began to catch on—to the consternation of the language lovers. The word was impossibly formed, said its detractors; it ought to be something like *rely-on-able*, since we don't *rely* a thing, but *rely on* it. Fitzedward Hall devoted an entire (though short) book to the subject, called *On English Adjectives in -able, with Special Reference to Reliable* (1877). But *reliable* was no anomaly; a number of established words were prospering despite their similarly unorthodox origins. Gilbert M. Tucker, in *Our Common Speech* (1895), admitted that *reliable* wasn't pretty. But, he asked, "can we afford to discard it because it is not handsome in appearance?" As for the "rely on" argument, he said, "any comment may safely be deferred until people begin saying *laugh-at-able, indispense-with-able,* and *unaccount-for-able*; the principle is the same."

Remit for **Send**. "On receiving your bill I will remit the money." Remit does not mean that; it means give back, yield up, relinquish, etc. It means, also, to cancel, as in the phrase, the remission of sins.

• • •

Many critics shared Bierce's aversion to *remit*, perhaps because of its commercial associations, but Robert Palfrey Utter defended it. "The facts do not bear out the assertion that *remit* should not be used in place of *send*," he wrote in *Every-Day Words and Their Uses* (1916). "It does not mean *send* in ordinary senses, but has the special meaning *to send money or valuables*." Since *remit* had been used that way since the 17th century, Utter was merely stating the obvious.

Rendition for **Interpretation**, or **Performance**. "The actor's rendition of the part was good." Rendition means a surrender, or a giving back.

• • •

Rendition also meant "translation," as in the *OED*'s example from 1659: "The most ancient interpreters [of the Bible] were divided in their renditions." From "translation" to "interpretation" to "performance" (of a song or role) is not a huge shift in sense, but the "performance" sense was a 19th-century American innovation, and thus was viewed with suspicion. American critics tried to limit *rendition* to the "surrender" sense, but in vain; in fact, it soon spread to Britain, and is now standard everywhere.

Reportorial. A vile word, improperly made. It assumes the Latinized spelling, "reportor." The Romans had not the word, for they were, fortunately for them, without the thing.

• • •

It's true that *reportorial*—a French borrowing with a Latin ending—is "improperly made," if you care about that sort of thing. It also suffers the disadvantage of American birth, in the 1780s. Not every critic condemned it; Alfred Ayres, whose usage judgments Bierce often echoes, used *reportorial* twice without apology in *The Verbalist* (1896). Bierce was always happy to knock his chosen profession, however, and *reportorial* provides a good excuse for a bit of journalistic self-hatred.

Repudiate for **Deny**. "He repudiated the accusation."

• • •

Repudiate, originally "to divorce or cast off a wife," had acquired more general senses by the 19th century, like "reject with denial" or "reject with abhorrence." Bryant 1870 banned the verb, and White 1870 called it "pretentious" as a substitute for "deny." But many critics would have allowed *repudiate* for an emphatic and outraged denial; since Bierce doesn't say what sort of accusation he has in mind, it's impossible to tell why he repudiates *repudiate*.

Reside for **Live**. "They reside in Hohokus." Stilted.

• • •

Bierce follows Bryant 1870 in forbidding *reside* and *residence* (below). And they have a point: If someone always used *reside* for *live*, that language would be stilted, and maybe pretentious too. But *reside* has its place in legal contexts, where it means "to live officially." It is also useful to writers who need an occasional alternative to *live*, as Bierce the journalist was surely aware.

Residence for **Dwelling**, or **House**. See *Mansion*.

Respect for **Way**, or **Matter**. "They were alike in that respect." The misuse comes of abbreviating: the sentence properly written might be, They were alike in respect of that—i.e., with regard to that. The word in the bad sense has even been pluralized: "In many respects it is admirable."

• • •

Bierce's preferred sense of "in respect of"—"in relation to" or "in regard to"—is the older one, but *respect* had also been used to mean "aspect" since the 15th century. The phrases Bierce disapproves of—"in many respects," "in that respect," and the like—date to the 16th century; they appear in the 1611 King James Bible, in Milton, and in the writings of many of Bierce's fellow usage mavens. Bierce even granted himself poetic license, in *The Devil's Dictionary*, to use the forbidden phrase in a verse about braggarts. "In this respect they're really like the hen," he wrote, and there's no reason in the world he shouldn't have.

Respective. "They went to their respective homes." The adjective here (if an adjective is thought necessary) should be several.

In the adverbial form the word is properly used in the sentence following: John and James are bright and dull, respectively. That is, John is bright and James dull.

. . .

Once again, we see Bierce hoping to limit a word's use to one specific context. But *respective* also meant "separate, several, particular," as it had since a 1646 law "for the Ordination of Ministers . . . within their respective Bounds," according to the *OED*. *Respectively* dates to 1626. Both adjective and adverb have been used in this way ever since.

Responsible. "The bad weather is responsible for much sickness." "His intemperance was responsible for his crime." Responsibility is not an attribute of anything but human beings, and few of these can respond, in damages or otherwise. Responsible is nearly synonymous with accountable and answerable, which, also, are frequently misused.

. . .

We still occasionally hear the argument that weather (and other impersonal forces) can't be "responsible," and Bierce may have been the man who said it first. The usage was a brand-new Americanism a century ago, and other dissenters joined Bierce's opposition, but the expression seems to be outlasting its critics. *AHD4* says *responsible* can be applied to things when the word means "being the source or cause of," as in "Faulty construction was responsible for the crash."

Restive for **Restless.** These words have directly contrary meanings; the dictionaries' disallowance of their identity would be something to be thankful for, but that is a dream.

. . .

In the late 19th century, usage writers took a close look at *restive* and decided it was being misused for *restless*. Balky horses were *restive*, said White 1870—"standing stubbornly still, not frisky." Fitzedward Hall 1872 replied that "the ordinary sense of the word has always been 'unruly,' 'intractable,' 'refractory,'" and gave examples from a long list of literary worthies.

Now as then, the words overlap considerably. The "subtle distinction," says *The American Heritage Guide to Contemporary Usage* (2005), is between *restive*, "impatient with restriction," and *restless*, "fidgety." But *restive* is often merely a synonym for *restless*. "Some critics lament this development," says Garner 2003, "but it seems irreversible."

Retire for **Go to Bed.** English of the "genteel" sort. See *Genteel.*

• • •

"Retire to rest" or "to bed" was a standard phrase from the mid-17th century on, and in the mid-18th it began to appear as simply *retired*, when the bedtime context was clear. Another century passed, and *retire*, to the sensitive Victorian ear, now seemed like a way of avoiding the word *bed.* "Don't talk about retiring, unless you would seem like a prig or a prurient prude," said White 1870. "A vulgar, but unfortunately very common, euphemism," said Schele de Vere 1871 of *retire.*

But William Archer, an Englishman who in 1899 published an account of his visit to the United States, was skeptical of their premise. "If, as is commonly alleged, Americans say 'retire' because they consider it indelicate to go to bed, the feeling and the expression are alike foolish," he wrote. "But I do not believe that either is at all common in America. On the other hand, one may retire for the night without going to bed. In the case of ladies especially, the interval between retiring and going to bed is reputed to be far from inconsiderable." If the word is accurate, he concluded, why not say *retire*?

Euphemism or not, *retire* would soon star in one of the century's advertising landmarks. In 1910, the Fisk Tire Co. registered the trademark for its picture of a pajama-clad boy holding a worn tire and a candle, with the slogan "Time to Re-Tire?" Bierce was a punster himself; perhaps the ad helped him look more kindly on the verb *retire*.

Rev. for The Rev. "Rev. Dr. Smith."

• • •

Reverend, the traditionalists say, is an adjective, and must be preceded by *the*. Edward S. Gould, in *Good English* (1867), showed readers what horrors would ensue if they abandoned the definite article: "At last annual meeting of Blank Book Society, honourable John Smith took the chair, assisted by reverend John Brown and venerable John White. The office of secretary would have been filled by late John Green, but for his decease."

But according to *MWDEU*, the "tradition" has long been ignored: "*Reverend* is in fact used as a title, and it is also used as a noun (and has been since the 17th century)." An Episcopal minister may be "the Rev. Mr. Alford," but in other denominations, style varies: "This is really a matter of etiquette rather than linguistic propriety, and the preference of the clergy involved should be taken into account," advises *MWDEU*. As for actual practice, in newspaper usage today, despite the stylebook mandates, "Rev. Alford" outnumbers "the Rev. Mr. Alford" by a substantial margin.

Reverence for Revere.

• • •

Some word mavens have claimed that *reverence* has more to do with showing awed respect, and *revere* with feeling it. That may be the distinction Bierce was getting at. Or he could have been trying, as he so often did, to neaten up the lexicon by limiting *reverence* to its role as a noun and letting *revere* alone do the work of the verb.

Ride for **Drive**. On horseback one does drive, and in a vehicle one does ride, but a distinction is needed here, as in England; so, here as there, we may profitably make it, riding in the saddle and driving in the carriage.

. . .

For half a century, the usage commentators had worried over the proper vocabulary for going out in a carriage; if the driver held the reins, was the passenger out for a *ride* or a *drive*? Mathews 1876 said that you weren't *driving* unless you were holding the reins. Gould 1867 found the whole discussion annoying: "The discrimination between the two words . . . which a pseudo-fashion has attempted to establish, both in England and in the United States, is mere pedantry." By the time Bierce cast his halfhearted vote, Ford's Model T was rolling off the production line, and few people would have cared which verbs the fashionable set chose for their horse-powered outings.

Roomer for **Lodger**. See *Bedder* and *Mealer*—if you can find them.

. . .

Bierce had made this joke twenty years earlier, and would recycle it once more in *The Devil's Dictionary*. But is it a good joke? We don't need his *mealer* because *boarder* is the word for someone provided with meals. But sometimes *lodger* really did mean just a "bedder"—someone paying for room but not board—and the word *roomer* makes that status unambiguous.

The *OED*'s earliest related citation, for the verb *room*, comes from an 1828 letter by Harriet Beecher Stowe: "She rooms with me, and is very interesting." The explicitly non-mealer sense of *roomer*, as used at Yale, dates from 1871: "*Roomer*, a word used by landladies to designate a lodger or occupant of a room who takes his meals elsewhere." Webster 1913 calls *roomer* colloquial, and that's probably Bierce's objection to it. But if you were the landlady or the cook, you'd want to distinguish your roomers from your boarders, colloquially or not.

Round for **About.** "They stood round." See *Around.*

Ruination for **Ruin.** Questionably derived and problematically needful.

. . .

"Mother says I shan't go to Boston; for she knows it will be the ruination of me," says a character in an 1851 short story by T. S. Arthur. Bierce labels the word's derivation "questionable," but *ruination* comes from *ruinate,* a Latin-derived verb that was common in the 16th and 17th centuries, according to the *OED.*

Ruination itself dates to the mid-17th century, but both verb and noun gradually declined; in Webster 1828 they were labeled "inelegant and obsolete." By the later part of the century, they'd been demoted to "dialectal" and "jocular," and we find Uncle Remus (quoted in *Modern Language Notes,* 1889) saying, "Hits de ruination er dis country." Bierce, who disliked dialect writing—"the talk of ignorant persons misusing their own language"—was predictably cool to the fallen *ruination.*

Run for **Manage,** or **Conduct.** Vulgar—hardly better than slang.

. . .

Run to mean "supervise, manage," "make to run," was an American invention, and much commented on. The *OED* quotes an 1864 report in London's *Daily Telegraph* on the versatility of the American usage: "You may 'run' anything—a railroad, a band, a school, a newspaper . . . or an administration." This sense of *run* was also relatively new, and popular in business language—defects that would have loomed large in Bierce's eyes.

His own trade got off more lightly, however. Bierce had no

harsh words for the journalistic use of *run* for "publish," though that was also an Americanism, and an even newer usage than the *run* he found so vulgar.

S

Say for **Voice.** "He had no say in determining the matter." **Vulgar.**

• • •

Say, the noun, was respectable British English—it dated to the 16th century—but at least one 19th-century critic thought "have a say" must be a home-grown barbarism. In his *Dictionary of Americanisms* (1848), John Russell Bartlett offered no objection to *say* alone, but he called "have a say" "a phrase in vulgar use."

We can't tell from Bierce's terse comment whether he's condemning the noun itself or only the phrase. The *OED*'s earliest citation, however, reveals "have a say" as thoroughly English and far from vulgar. It appears in a commentary on the Apostles' Creed written by Thomas Jackson, later dean of Peterborough Cathedral, in 1614: "Shall they therefore have no saye at all in deciding controversies?"

Scholar for **Student,** or **Pupil.** A scholar is a person who is learned, not a person who is learning.

• • •

The earliest meaning of *scholar,* from the 11th century, was "young pupil"; it had shared that sense with the others—"university student," "learned person"—for centuries. But certain American scholars, in the 19th century, began to chafe at sharing the title with children just learning the alphabet. Ayres 1896 quoted approvingly from a Philadelphia newspaper: "It would be a reform in the use of the word if *scholar* could be limited to learned persons."

Vizetelly 1906 simply declared that the sense of the word had changed: *Scholar* now meant someone "distinguished for the pursuit and possession of knowledge," and was too "high-sounding" a word for a mere pupil.

In England, however, there was no discomfort with the notion of young scholars: Fowler, in *The King's English* (1906), used the sample sentence "The master beat the scholar with a strap."

Score for **Win, Obtain**, etc. "He scored an advantage over his opponent." To score is not to win a point, but to record it.

• • •

Score's many senses begin with the noun meaning "mark, notch," and in the 18th century the verb had Bierce's preferred meaning, "record a point." But in the mid-19th century, *score* began to be used of winning the point as well. By 1870, the *New York Times* was using *score* to mean "make a run" in baseball: "The Athletics went to the bat, scoring six runs." Bierce might not have liked that example—he once called spectator sports "the last shifts of intellectual vacuity"—but as a newspaperman, he had to know that "scoring runs" was standard sporting English. He was just being contrary.

Second-handed for **Second-hand**. There is no such word.

• • •

Second-handed is "an old formation," says Utter in *Every-Day Words and Their Uses* (1916); it's chiefly dialect, says the *OED* (Robert Burns used it). Usage books barely mention it after the 1920s, and *secondhand*, as both adjective and adverb, is far more common. But it wasn't (and isn't) true that "there is no such word."

Secure for **Procure**. "He secured a position as book-keeper." "The dwarf secured a stick and guarded the jewels that he had found." Then it was the jewels that were secured.

• • •

The sense of *secure* that Bierce dislikes—"to get hold or possession of (something desirable) as the result of effort or contrivance"— dates to 1743, according to the *OED*. Since it represents only a slight extension of the verb's earlier senses, "make secure, certain, safe"— as in the Constitution's "to secure the blessings of liberty"—it seems odd to quibble about it, and apparently no one but Bierce ever did.

Seldom ever. A most absurd locution.

· · ·

The phrase *seldom ever* (meaning "seldom if ever") is a thousand years old, notes *MWDEU*: "Like it or not, it is a well-aged idiom." Bierce and his fellow usagists did not like it. Robert Palfrey Utter, in *Every-Day Words and Their Uses* (1916), summed up the prevailing view: "The phrases *seldom if ever* and *seldom or never* mean essentially the same thing and are both in good use. *Seldom ever* is said to be obsolete and *seldom or ever* is illogical, a mere confusion of the other two." But *seldom ever* was not, and is not, obsolete; it may be absurd, but it's still used around the world.

Self-confessed. "A self-confessed assassin." Self is superfluous: one's sins cannot be confessed by another.

· · ·

Bierce is correct, of course; to "confess" is to speak of oneself. But *self-confessed*, perhaps because it was more emphatic than mere *confessed*, had been spreading in England and America since the early 19th century. Even Bierce was swept along by the current: "The person who complains of 'the tyranny of fashion' is a self-confessed fool," he wrote in 1895. And he left that *self-confessed* unchanged in his *Collected Works*, published several years after this denunciation in *Write It Right*.

Sensation for Emotion. "The play caused a great sensation." "A sensational newspaper." A sensation is a physical feeling; an emotion, a mental. Doubtless the one usually accompanies the other, but the good writer will name the one that he has in mind, not the other. There are few errors more common than the one here noted.

. . .

Bierce's example seems carelessly phrased—he couldn't have meant that we should say "The play caused a great emotion" or "an emotional newspaper." In any case, *sensation* and *emotion* were blending in sense by the mid-18th century, and *sensation* meaning "collective excitement" had debuted by 1779. The *OED* quotes Southey and Dickens using the word, and Macaulay, in 1855: "The sensation produced by this work was immense." Even the later use of *sensation* to mean the event or person causing the excitement—"she was a sensation in the role"—was half a century old by the time Bierce lodged his protest. "There are few errors more common," says Bierce; a judgment like that usually means the "error" is no longer erroneous.

Sense for Smell. "She sensed the fragrance of roses." Society English.

. . .

If "society English" favored the expression "sense the fragrance," it left no evidence in print. But as *MWDEU* points out, except for *aroma*, "words associated with olfactory sensations tend to acquire less pleasant connotations over time." Bierce's sharp nose may have caught a whiff of suspicion, somewhere in the air, about the decorousness of *smell*.

Set for Sit. "A setting hen."

. . .

Since the 15th century, to *set* a hen has meant to "put her to sit upon eggs"; since the 16th century, perhaps not surprisingly, hens have been said to both *sit* and *set* on their eggs. "Hens do not *set*," said White 1870. "They *sit*, as the court does, and frequently to better purpose." But *set* has remained common in chicken-and-egg contexts, and Bernstein 1965 listed it as one of two exceptions to the rule: "The sun *sets* (intransitive) and the hen *sets*."

Settee for **Settle.** This word belongs to the peasantry of speech.

. . .

What's wrong with *settee*? Perhaps in Bierce's America the word seemed pompous, like *mansion* and *residence*. As Bierce hints, *settee* may be a variant of *settle*, mysteriously endowed with that double-*e* suffix. (In *goatee* and *settee*, "the analogies that may have given rise to the suffix are uncertain," says the *OED*.)

Settee appeared in print in London as early as 1716, and it may simply have been out of fashion by the time Bierce encountered it. The author of *Suffolk Words* (1823), a regional dialect guide, defined *settee* as "a sopha or moveable window-seat; in more modern language called, I believe, conversation stool. I have not heard the word of many years, and believe it is going out." If it was "going out," though, it has now come back; the *Columbia Guide to Standard American English* (1993) calls *settee* standard, along with *sofa, couch, davenport, settle,* and other sorts of seating. *Conversation stool,* however, is not on the list.

Settle for **Pay.** "Settle the bill." "I shall take it now and settle for it later."

. . .

Since the phrase "settle accounts" dates to the 17th century, it seems natural enough that by the early 19th century one could speak of "settling a bill." The expression appeared on both sides of the Atlantic in official documents and in popular novels: "Your uncle has gone to settle our bill" (*The Travellers*, by Catharine

Maria Sedgwick, 1825); "If you'll have the kindness to settle that little bill of mine, I'll thank you" (*The Pickwick Papers*, by Charles Dickens, 1838).

But literal-minded critics like White 1870 argued that though you may *settle* ("adjust, fix") an account, you do not settle a bill when you are simply paying it; the verb was not only inaccurate, White suggested, but pretentious as well. Vizetelly 1906 shared White's disdain: "Do not speak of *settling* a bill unless there is some matter in dispute concerning it," he ordered. By 1917, however, J. Lesslie Hall, in *English Usage*, could report that "five dictionaries and four reputable authors" approved of *settle*. "Polite colloquial usage favors it considerably," he concluded.

Shades for **Shade.** "Shades of Noah! how it rained!" "O shades of Caesar!" A shade is a departed soul, as conceived by the ancients; one to each mortal part is the proper allowance.

· · ·

To Bierce, "shades of Noah" was as nonsensical as "Great Caesar's ghosts!" would be to us. But this particular use of *shade*—"in humorous invocation of the spirit of a deceased person, as likely to be horrified or amazed by some action or occurrence," as the OED glosses it—was broadening, over the 19th century, into plural and loose usage. Eventually *shade* referred merely to "some person or thing in the past of which a present event is reminiscent." The 20th-century examples in the OED have this relaxed sense: "I have just had my ninth snifter of Scotch. O shades of Bert Savoy!" (Hart Crane, 1928). And the headline "Shades of 1918?" on a 2009 report about influenza is obviously invoking the memory of the great flu epidemic itself, not the spirits of the departed.

Show for **Chance,** or **Opportunity.** "He didn't stand a show." Say, He had no chance.

· · ·

An 1890 slang dictionary calls this sense of *show* American, but adds that it has become "one of the commonest of slang words in Australia." *Show* doesn't appear to have survived Bierce's blacklisting.

Sick for Ill. Good usage now limits this word to cases of nausea, but it is still legitimate in sickly, sickness, love-sick, and the like.

• • •

The consensus on "good usage" was not as firm as Bierce suggests. The British had largely restricted the sense of *sick* to "nauseated," but Americans were resisting. White 1870 said the British had "perverted" the senses of *sick* and *ill;* Ayres 1881 called *sick* "the stronger word, and ordinarily the better word." And J. Lesslie Hall, in *English Usage* (1917), firmly rejected the change. "The word *sick* in its wide meaning is as old as the language," he said. "It is familiar to every reader of Shakespeare and of Bible English. From the days of James I to the present it has been one of the most frequent words in both colloquial and literary English. The recent objection to it is absolutely unaccountable and absolutely unreasonable—linguistic squeamishness." The British continue to opt for squeamishness, but most Americans were, and are, comfortable with the word *sick.*

Side for Agree, or Stand. "I side with the Democrats." "He always sided with what he thought right."

• • •

Did Bierce think "side with" was a lowly Americanism? It wasn't; it dates to 1600, and it showed up in the writings of Shakespeare, Pope, and zealous English-language regulator Jonathan Swift, who used it in its negative form: "The equitable part of those who now side against the court, will probably be more temperate" (1738).

Sideburns for Burnsides. A form of whiskers named from a noted general of the civil war, Ambrose E. Burnside. It seems to be thought that the word side has something to do with it, and that as an adjective it should come first, according to our idiom.

. . .

General Burnside, known as a so-so commander but a nice guy, wore a mustache that flowed into a huge pair of muttonchop side-whiskers above a clean-shaven chin. This "Burnside" style was transformed into *sideburns*, perhaps to match *side-whiskers*, and the neologism spread rapidly in the last quarter of the 19th century. Burnside, however, was not totally forgotten: His role in the language was celebrated in a Burma Shave–style verse in Keith Preston's 1929 collection of prose and poetry, *Pot Shots from Pegasus.*

> *A small thing oft oblivion's tide turns;*
> *Burnside's remembered for his sideburns,*
> *While generals greater but less hairy*
> *To-day have grown inglorious, very.*

Side-hill for **Hillside.** A reasonless transposition for which it is impossible to assign a cause, unless it is abbreviated from side o' the hill.

. . .

Hurd 1847 didn't like *side-hill* either; Bartlett 1877 thought it was an Americanism, and perhaps Bierce did too, though the word had appeared in both Britain and America. Thoreau, in *The Maine Woods*, wrote of arriving "upon a side-hill, or rather side-mountain," and in American usage the word is "chiefly Northern, esp. North East," according to the *Dictionary of American Regional English.*

Sidehill also has several specialized uses; a golf blog, for example, offers Tiger Woods's "tips for side-hill lies." Sidehill plows date to the 1830s, and a modern harvester can be equipped with a sidehill leveling system. And let's not forget the sidehill badger, the mythical creature equipped for its sloping environment with legs that are shorter on the uphill side; "hillside badger" wouldn't sound nearly as exotic.

Sideways for **Sidewise**. See *Endways*.

Since for **Ago**. "He came here not long since and died."

. . .

A few usage writers tried to make trouble over "long since." Ayres 1881 said *since* required a following clause, as in "since I saw you," so "I saw him not long since" was incorrect. Other critics proposed that "long since" should be limited to recent events, "long ago" reserved for distant ones.

But the idiom had been standard for some four hundred years and was widespread among educated speakers, including language mavens. Alford 1864 mentioned "a leading article of the Times, not long since"; White 1870 wrote, "only a few days since, as I spoke of riding to a British friend"; Newton and Denney 1900 offered the sample sentence "The train left an hour since," and assured their young readers that "This use of since is correct."

Smart for **Bright**, or **Able**. An Americanism that is dying out. But "smart" has recently come into use for fashionable, which is almost as bad.

. . .

Bierce really didn't get *smart*. It is not in fact an Americanism; its first recorded use in the "clever" sense, in 1628, is British. By Bierce's time it was indeed more common in America than Britain, but his claim that it was "dying out" was sheer wishful thinking. *Smart* meaning "fashionable"—also British usage—had been voguish since the 1880s among the kind of people Bierce scorned, and that would have been enough to damn it in his eyes. See *Brainy*.

Snap for **Period** (of time) or **Spell.** "A cold snap." This is a word of incomprehensible origin in that sense; we can know only that its parents were not respectable. "Spell" is itself not very well-born.

• • •

A "cold snap" is no more incomprehensible than a "biting wind," and *snap* is a fine old Germanic word, but this sense of *snap* is apparently an American innovation: The *OED*'s earliest example dates from 1740, when the journals of the Rev. Thomas Smith and the Rev. Samuel Deane of Maine recorded "two or three snaps of cold weather." The word's American heritage and its informal tone are, of course, two of Bierce's least favorite things. (As for *spell*, it is first recorded in England in the 16th century; its "period of time" sense is rooted in *spell* meaning "a turn, shift, or relay.")

So—as. See **As—as.**

So for **True.** "If you see it in the Daily Livercomplaint it is so." "Is that so?" Colloquial and worse.

• • •

What could Bierce have seen in this usage that would make him call it "colloquial and worse"? "It is so," meaning "it is thus," appears in King Alfred's writing (888), in *Beowulf* (1000), and in the King James Bible (1611): "If the dew be on the fleece only . . . And it was so." Lord North wrote to King George III, warning of bad news from the colonies, "which, if it is so, shews . . . how impossible it is to obtain peace." *It is so* is found in Shakespeare and Trollope, Edmund Burke and Mark Twain. But Bierce knew what he liked, and he didn't like "it is so."

Solemnize. This word rightly means to make solemn, not to perform, or celebrate, ceremoniously something already solemn, as a marriage, or a mass. We have no exact synonym, but this explains, rather than justifies, its use.

. . .

There's a reason Bierce is the only peevologist to have complained about *solemnize*: He's wrong. The verb has meant "celebrate ceremoniously" since its English debut in the 14th century. The *OED*'s earliest reference is from a 1382 Wyclif Bible: "There is not solemnized such a Passover in Israel, from the times of Samuel" (spelling modernized). The sense Bierce preferred—"to make solemn"—is also current, but it didn't turn up till the 18th century. And why did he prefer it? We may never know.

Some for Somewhat. "He was hurt some."

. . .

The adverbial *some*, allegedly short for *somewhat*, had been disparaged at least since John Russell Bartlett's judgment in *A Dictionary of Americanisms* (1848): "Used chiefly by the illiterate." But though one use of *some*—"she's some better"—is dialectal, the one Bierce cites is standard informal American. *MWDEU*'s examples include "I've been brooding some" (E. B. White, of Strunk and White fame), "she wept some" (Faulkner), and "he also helped out some" (Calvin Trillin). In these constructions, says *MWDEU*, "you need not (and sometimes cannot) automatically replace [*some*] with *somewhat*."

Soon for Willingly. "I would as soon go as stay." "That soldier would sooner eat than fight." Say, rather eat.

. . .

Most other usagists ignore this use of *soon*, and rightly; it is standard and very old. The *OED* cites *soon* for "willingly" from the 13th century on, and *sooner* for "rather" from the 15th century. Shakespeare used it in *Julius Caesar* ("I do not know the man I should avoyd So soone as that spare Cassius"), and Fielding in *Tom Jones* ("I would sooner starve than take any reward for betraying your Ladyship"). Webster 1828 and 1913 both approve the sense as current, and the only other objection of the period appears (with no explanation) in a commercial-school handbook. Bierce doesn't say so, but his record suggests he would like to see *sooner* used only of time, not volition.

Space for **Period.** "A long space of time." Space is so different a thing from time that the two do not go well together.

• • •

If Bierce had been reading physics, instead of news of the war in Mexico, he might have heard of "the space-time manifold of relativity" before he disappeared around the end of 1913. If he had lived another few years, the *OED* would have published the *S* volume, showing that *space* had meant "duration, period" even before it meant "extent, area," and that both senses were current in the 14th century. Bierce being Bierce, he would probably have concluded that 14th-century English needed a good editor; but "space of time" is so natural that even Bierce, not surprisingly, used expressions like "a moment's space" in his published work.

Spend for **Pass.** "We shall spend the summer in Europe." Spend denotes a voluntary relinquishment, but time goes from us against our will.

• • •

Certainly time passes without our approval, though "against our will" is an odd way to put it. But speakers of English have been "spending time"—a metaphor that implies not that they control its passing, but that they can choose what they do with it—since 1300 or so. Did Bierce think *spend* had the commercial taint he found so distasteful? He wasn't saying.

Square for **Block**. "He lives three squares away." A city block is seldom square.

. . .

The objection is bizarrely literal, since the *square* in a town center or city neighborhood is seldom a perfect square. But Bierce seems to have been provoked by Philadelphia's continuing to call its city blocks *squares* even when other once-"squared" metropolises had switched to calling them *blocks*.

Squirt for **Spurt**. Absurd.

. . .

Squirt is actually older than *spurt*, and both verbs are equally respectable. Bierce's distaste may have been fueled by the 19th-century slang uses of *squirt*, the noun; Bartlett 1848 defines *squirt* as "a foppish young fellow; a whipper-snapper," and calls it a vulgar Americanism. Later, *squirt* was college slang for a piece of showy prose, and of course there were squirt guns. Undignified associations like those might well have sullied the verb, and not only for the hypersensitive Bierce.

Stand and **Stand for** for **Endure**. "The patient stands pain well." "He would not stand for misrepresentation."

. . .

It begins to sound as if Bierce was running out of real language disputes and just padding his book with any quirky peeve he could think up. There is no plausible reason to dislike *stand* for "put up with," a 17th-century extension of the verb that was used by Steele, Scott, Carlyle, and Conrad—to mention only writers Bierce might have read.

Standpoint for **Point of View,** or **Viewpoint.**

• • •

Standpoint and *viewpoint* were both new in the 19th century, but Americans were familiar with *point of view,* in use since about 1700, and thus were prepared for *viewpoint. Standpoint* was a tougher sell, though it came straight from the German *standpunkt.* Edward S. Gould, in a confused but fierce analysis, declared it "not English." "'Stand,' by itself, is English," he admitted in *Good English* (1867), "and 'point,' by itself, is English: but the two words, like certain chemical ingredients, will not unite until a combining medium is introduced."

Further denunciations followed, but within a couple of decades, the dispute had evaporated. "This useful word has recently established itself in the language," said Scott and Denney 1900. "It has been censured," said Utter 1916, "but must be admitted as good usage." And *standpoint* lived happily ever after.

State for **Say.** "He stated that he came from Chicago." "It is stated that the president is angry." We state a proposition, or a principle, but say that we are well. And we say our prayers—some of us.

• • •

It's universally deplored, and maybe overdone by journalists and beginning writers, but is using *state* for *say* really a common stylistic sin? *MWDEU* suggests that the critics were overreacting; in edited prose, *state* is generally used as Bierce recommends, "to imply a formal, precise, or emphatic declaration or report." See *Declared.*

Still Continue. "The rain still continues." Omit still; it is contained in the other word.

• • •

Here's another case for the pleonasm police, who call this a flagrant usage crime. But *still* is not necessarily redundant in such usage, where it emphasizes the unusual persistence of whatever it is that won't stop.

And *still continue* is such natural English that even the usagists use it. Robert Lowth, the 18th-century grammarian and bishop of London—perhaps influenced by the cadences of the Bible, which he translated—wrote *still continue* several times. ("The Israelites . . . have so long marvellously subsisted, and still continue to subsist, as a people.")

Roscoe Mongan's *Practical English Grammar* (1864), illustrating the present perfect, has, "we cannot say, 'Cromwell *has founded* a dynasty;' because that dynasty does not still continue." Lounsbury's *Standard of Usage in English* (1908) refers to "books which in some cases still continue to have a fairly respectable sale."

Stock. "I take no stock in it." Disagreeably commercial. Say, I have no faith in it. Many such metaphorical expressions were unobjectionable, even pleasing, in the mouth of him who first used them, but by constant repetition by others have become mere slang, with all the offensiveness of plagiarism. The prime objectionableness of slang is its hideous lack of originality. Until mouth-worn it is not slang.

• • •

If you don't like an expression, any reason will do; thus "take no stock" is called worn-out, tired, clichéd. But *stunt*, below, was newly hatched, yet it too is labeled "overworked." And *dilapidated*—a wonderful metaphor of a word, according to Trench 1852—should not be "worked" at all, except literally, says Bierce. Which only shows that he was no more hobbled by consistency than any other prescriptivist.

Stop for Stay. "Prayer will not stop the ravages of cholera." Stop is frequently misused for stay in another sense of the latter

word: "He is stopping at the hotel." Stopping is not a continuing act; one cannot be stopping who has already stopped.

· · ·

Nineteenth-century writers used both "stop the ravages" and "stay
the ravages," and only Bierce seems to have registered a preference in that case. But *stop* meaning "stop over, stay" was universally opposed. Ayres 1881 is typical: " 'Where are you *stopping*?' 'At
the Metropolitan.' The proper word to use here is *staying. To stop*
means to cease to go forward." *Stop* is still used for *stay*, especially
in England, but the *Concise Oxford English Dictionary* labels it informal even there.

Stunt. A word recently introduced and now overworked, meaning a task, or performance in one's trade, or calling,—doubtless
a variant of stint, without that word's suggestion of allotment
and limitation. It is still in the reptilian stage of evolution.

· · ·

Stunt was indeed recent—the first *OED* example, dated 1878,
refers to "a stunt for advertising the books." And it's not impossible (though far from certain) that the word was derived from *stint*.
But Bierce seems to have missed its other meaning—a vaudeville
"turn" or some similar physical feat—and that's the one that survived the reptilian stage to become the dominant sense.

Subsequent for **Later**, or **Succeeding**. Legitimate enough, but
ugly and needless. "He was subsequently hanged." Say, afterward.

· · ·

Bierce's fellow commentators—mostly scholars, not journalists,
and thus more tolerant of big words—used *subsequent* freely. A
few later critics called it stuffy, and it is certainly formal. But *subsequent* has its place; it can imply not only that something comes
later, notes *MWDEU*, but that it "in some way grows out of or is
closely connected with what precedes it."

Substantiate for **Prove**. Why?

• • •

Why? Because sometimes even Ambrose Bierce needs the longer word, as he did for his poem "The Lawyer," printed at the *authentic* entry in *The Devil's Dictionary*:

> He ne'er discredited authentic news,
> That tended to substantiate his views . . .

Success. "The project was a success." Say, was successful. Success should not have the indefinite article.

• • •

As the plural *successes* dated to 1666, the emergence of a singular *success* in the late 18th century—as in "the operation was a success"—should not have been unexpected. But this concrete sense of *success*, referring not to the abstract concept ("success is sweet") but to a person or phenomenon that succeeds, took off only in Bierce's adulthood, in the late 19th century. Scott and Denney 1900 labeled it disputed usage, but commented that "*A success* is used by the best writers."

Such Another for **Another Such**. There is illustrious authority for this—in poetry. Poets are a lawless folk, and may do as they please so long as they do please.

• • •

In his 1852 book *On the Study of Words*, Richard Chenevix Trench himself used the phrase "such another [man]." Henry H. Breen, in *Modern English Literature* (1857), wrote, "It would be difficult to crowd into the limited compass of six lines such another combination of ignorance, absurdity, unfounded assumption," etc. But by the end of that decade, everyone in the usage trade had agreed that *another such* was the correct expression, and *such another* was wrong—and that was that.

Such for **So.** "He had such weak legs that he could not stand." The absurdity of this is made obvious by changing the form of the statement: "His legs were such weak that he could not stand." If the word is an adverb in the one sentence it is in the other. "He is such a great bore that none can endure him." Say, so great a bore.

. . .

Bierce is repeating the argument of Ayres 1881 that "such weak legs" is equivalent to "legs such weak." The analysis hasn't a leg to stand on; why should *such* and *so* be expected to function interchangeably? The "such weak legs" construction dates to the early 16th century, according to the *OED*, and was used by Shakespeare ("such fierce alarums"), Scott ("such early years"), and Dickens ("such great dilapidation"), among many others.

Suicide. This is never a verb. "He suicided." Say, He killed himself, or He took his own life. See *Commit Suicide.*

. . .

Garner 2003 calls *to suicide* "trendy and semiliterate," and it has never had much of a constituency, yet it has been edging into the language since the mid-19th century. Why do we see this verb, but no "he fratricided" or "the gardener herbicided"? Not trendiness, perhaps, as much as the universal desire to name a taboo subject as briefly and delicately as possible.

Supererogation. To supererogate is to overpay, or to do more than duty requires. But the excess must be in the line of duty; merely needless and irrelevant action is not supererogation. The word is not a natural one, at best.

. . .

History has seconded Bierce's skepticism about the word; it isn't often, I'd guess, that an editor has to cross out *supererogation* and substitute something more "natural."

Sure for **Surely.** "They will come, sure." Slang.

· · ·

Milton used both *sure* and *surely* as adverbs, notes *MWDEU*—"God sure esteems the growth . . . of one virtuous person" (1644)—and they were interchangeable well into the 18th century. Then adverbial *sure* began to fade from British usage, and in the later 19th century, Americans started feeling uncertain about it as well.

But adverbial *sure* has not become mere slang; instead, says *MWDEU*, we've established a stylistic split between *sure* and *surely*. The first is prevalent in speech and informal writing: "The Iranians sure have a way of bringing out the worst in us" (*Newsweek*, 1986). The second is more elevated and more tentative: "Surely . . . they can get a visa in Tehran" (*Tower Commission Report*, 1987). Surely few Americans find these conventions confusing.

Survive for **Live,** or **Persist.** Survival is an outliving, or outlasting of something else. "The custom survives" is wrong, but a custom may survive its utility. Survive is a transitive verb.

· · ·

It is true that *survive* means "outlive," and Bierce has decided, apparently on his own authority, that whatever is outlived must be stated as a direct object. But that was never true; *survive* was recorded as an intransitive verb in 1473, a century before its first transitive use. The verb can mean "outlive another," says the *OED*, but it can also mean to live after "some event (expressed or implied)," or even simply "to live on": "Many children borne the seventh month survive and do well" (1615).

Sustain for **Incur.** "He sustained an injury." "He sustained a broken neck." That means that although his neck was broken he did not yield to the mischance.

· · ·

Henry Alford was an unlikely leader for the herd of usage mavens denouncing "sustain an injury." In his years at Cambridge University, he might have noticed that *sustain* could mean not just "support" but also "suffer, undergo"—but he must have been reading his Greek instead. In *The Queen's English* (1864) he called this use of *sustain* a journalistic pomposity, and his fellow critics followed along meekly. Later commentators, having learned from the OED that the usage dated to circa 1400, found new reasons to disapprove, but *sustain* is thriving nonetheless. Garner 2003 calls it officialese, and perhaps it is sometimes journalese, but it hardly deserves the bashing it has sustained.

T

Talented for Gifted. These are both past participles, but there was once the verb to gift, whereas there was never the verb "to talent." If Nature did not talent a person the person is not talented.

· · ·

Dozens of other adjectives had been formed, like *talented*, from nouns rather than verbs, but *talented* was a relative upstart in Bierce's day, and still unwelcome in traditional circles. It had its defenders, though: "Fault is perpetually found with *talented*, on the ground that participles ought not to be formed from nouns," wrote Gilbert M. Tucker in *Our Common Speech* (1895). "But a tongue that already includes *diseased, gifted, lettered, bigoted, turreted, landed, skilled*, [etc.] . . . will hardly suffer much by admitting other formations of the same kind." See *Landed, Moneyed*.

Tantamount for **Equivalent**. "Apology is tantamount to confession." Let this ugly word alone; it is not only illegitimate, but ludicrously suggests catamount.

. . .

It's "illegitimate," presumably, because it's derived from a verb phrase, the French *tant amunter*, "to amount to as much"—though we can only guess, since other usage writers don't object to it. *Tantamount*'s adoption as an adjective in the 17th century may have been influenced by *paramount*, but it's not likely *catamount* was involved; that association is Bierce's own strange imagination at work.

Tasty for **Tasteful**. Vulgar.

. . .

Starting in the mid-18th century, *tasty* had a brief run as an acceptable variant of *tasteful*; there were tasty people, tasty hairstyles, and tasty pieces of furniture. By the early 19th century, Samuel Taylor Coleridge was wearying of the fad: *Tasty* had been worn out, he said, by "milliners, tailors, and . . . dandies." And by 1869, Richard Meade Bache was declaring it done for: "Although the words *tasty* and *tastily* have been used by some good writers, they have at present a decidedly vulgar twang." When Bierce added his parting shot forty years later, *tasty* had already retreated from the fashionable world to its home in the kitchen.

Tear Down for **Pull Down**. "The house was torn down." This is an indigenous solecism; they do not say so in England.

. . .

Nobody else was distressed by this minor divergence of idioms, but it had irked Bierce for years. In a dialogue reprinted in the *Writer* magazine in 1903, Bierce's Melancholy Author asked his interviewer, the Timorous Reporter, "Why do [Americans] say 'tear' down a building, instead of 'pull' down? A building is not a textile fabric. A tent is, but that is not said to be 'torn' down; it is 'taken' down." (The Timorous Reporter, needless to say, had no answer.)

Than Whom. See *Whom*. "George Washington, than whom there was no greater man, loved a jest." The misuse of whom after than is almost universal.*

· · ·

Than whom constitutes its own little grammar footnote, perhaps because Milton famously wrote, in *Paradise Lost*, "Beelzebub . . . than whom, Satan except, none higher sat." For the grammarians who insist that *than* is only a conjunction, not a preposition, Milton was wrong: It should have been "than who . . . none higher sat" (because it's "None higher sat *than he*"). But *than whom* sounded right to Milton in 1667, as it had to writers a century before him.

How to justify Milton's grammar to grammarians? Some critics, as early as the 18th century, thought *than* should be recognized as a preposition. The conjunction faction, however, decided it was simpler just to declare *than whom* a special case. The phrase became an "invariable construction," the *OED* explains, "which is universally accepted instead of *than who*." Well, *almost* universally accepted . . .

The. A little word that is terribly overworked. It is needlessly affixed to names of most diseases: "the cholera," "the smallpox," "the scarlet fever," and such. Some escape it: we do not say, "the sciatica," nor "the locomotor ataxia." It is too common in general propositions, as, "The payment of interest is the payment of debt." "The virtues that are automatic are the best." "The tendency to falsehood should be checked." "Kings are not under the control of the law." It is impossible to note here all

---

* These two sentences were originally part of Bierce's *Whom* entry; they've been moved to *Than Whom* for ease of reading.

forms of this misuse, but a page of almost any book will supply abundant instance. We do not suffer so abject slavery to the definite article as the French, but neither do we manifest their spirit of rebellion by sometimes cutting off the oppressor's tail. One envies the Romans, who had no article, definite or indefinite.

. . .

"The ague" and "the cholera" were considered common, vulgar expressions in Bierce's time. But the problems with his sample sentences are not so clear. Which *the*s are superfluous, and why? Fitzgerald 1901 also thought there were too many *the*s: "Why should we not say 'engaged in study of antiquities,' as we say, 'engaged in study'?" he asked.

Were these two anticipating the 1923 birth of *Time* magazine, whose breathless prose would shed *the*s like dandruff, recasting "Jake Flake, the flamboyant bronco buster," as "Flamboyant Bronco Buster Jake Flake"? It seems unlikely. Fitzgerald may have been protesting Victorian elegantisms like "the dance" and "the opera" (and "the study of"), but Bierce's reasoning remains obscure.

The Following. "Washington wrote the following." The following what? Put in the noun. "The following animals are ruminants." It is not the animals that follow, but their names.

. . .

According to Bierce, "the following are ruminants" is wrong; "the following animals are ruminants" is also wrong. Would "the animals whose names follow are ruminants" satisfy him?

The "absolute" use of *the following*, despite Bierce's antipathy, is standard English. It appeared in Robert Lowth's important early work *A Short Introduction to English Grammar* (1763): "The following seem to have lost the *en* of the Participle." Schele de Vere 1871 used it, and so did Ransom 1911: "Avoid the mixed construction involved in the following," he instructed in *Hints & "Don'ts" for Writers and Copyreaders*. The first part of Bierce's objection is baseless; the second is a product of the literalism that hears a usage crime in "His name is Mr. Smith."

The Same. "They cooked the flesh of the lion and ate the same." "An old man lived in a cave, and the same was a cripple." In humorous composition this may do, though it is not funny; but in serious work use the regular pronoun.

· · ·

The use of *same* instead of a pronoun dates to the 14th century, says the *OED*, and was normal English for Spenser, Shakespeare, and the editors of the King James Bible: "He that shall endure unto the end, the same shall be saved." Sometime in the 19th century, though, it fell out of favor. Henry H. Breen, in *Modern English Literature* (1857), complained that the usage "has gradually encroached upon the domain of ordinary prose, usurping the rights of the legitimate pronouns . . . You can hardly turn a sentence without falling foul of its prim little figure."

The same has never been the same. Fowler 1926 banned it from good usage; Bernstein 1965 called it a casualism, "to be used only with semihumorous intent"; Garner 2003 calls it pretentious. But *MWDEU* thinks *same* is unfairly abused, and offers a sampling of respected writers who have used the word. Among them is E. B. White, for whom "semi-humorous" must have been good enough; in a 1967 letter, he wrote of "the joy of life and the terror of same."

Then as an Adjective. "The then governor of the colony." Say, the governor of the colony at that time.

· · ·

Sir Philip Sidney mentioned "the then duke of Northumberland" in 1584, and the usage has been standard ever since. A couple of other critics, before and after Bierce, have turned up their noses at it, but most usagists—and most writers—think it's fine. J. Lesslie

Hall defended it as "concise and convenient" in *English Usage* (1917), and mentioned Johnson, Byron, Ruskin, and Trollope among writers who have used it.

Those Kind for **That Kind.** "Those kind of things." Almost too absurd for condemnation, and happily not very common out of the class of analphabets.

· · ·

Alford 1864 explained the phrase "those kind of things" as a mistake due to what Greek grammar calls the law of attraction. "If an important noun in a sentence is in a certain case, say the genitive or dative, a relative pronoun referring to it is put in the same case, though by the construction of the sentence it ought to be in another." Likewise, he said, in "this kind of things," or "that kind of things," the pronoun should be singular; but the plural noun *things* "gives a plural complexion to the whole," so we often say "these kind" or "those kind" of things, instead of "this kind" or "that kind."

Alford's analysis—and the occurrence of "these kind" in Sidney, Shakespeare, and Milton—didn't stop critics from trying to clean up the public's usage. But according to *MWDEU*, these kinds (and *sorts* and *types*) of mismatched constructions "have been in use since the 18th century or earlier." And their stigma has eased, if only slightly; Bierce thought *those kind* was an illiteracy, but Garner 2003 calls it merely slovenly.

Though for **If.** "She wept as though her heart was broken." Many good writers, even some devoid of the lexicographers' passion for inclusion and approval, have specifically defended this locution, backing their example by their precept. Perhaps it is a question of taste; let us attend their cry and pass on.

· · ·

Bierce cheats by labeling this entry "Though for If," as if the words, not the phrases *as though* and *as if*, are the issue. Ayres

1896 did something similar, taking apart a sentence with *as though* to show that it can't possibly work: It would be "The man moves *as* he would move *though* he were tired." This is pointless fiddling; *as though* is an idiom, and one that, as Utter 1916 noted, "has been continuously in good use for at least six centuries [make that seven], and shows no signs of going out of favor."

Thrifty for Thriving. "A thrifty village." To thrive is an end; thrift is a means to that end.

• • •

We now make the distinction Bierce urged, but *thrifty*, before it came to mean "economical," was a synonym for *thriving*. The usage was still current, though fading, in the 19th century: Webster 1828 and 1913 both listed the "thriving" sense for *thrifty*, "as, a thrifty plant or colt."

Through for Done. "The lecturer is through talking." "I am through with it." Say, I have done with it.

• • •

"I am through" had sprung up only in the 19th century, and it was viewed with some suspicion. *Through* "in the sense of have finished is an Americanism," said Ayres 1896. "The locution 'I am through' is seldom heard in Great Britain." But unlike the resistance to "I am done," which simmered throughout the 20th century and still has its adherents, hostility to "I am through" was short-lived. The usage is now standard; in fact, notes Garner 2003, "many stylists prefer *through*" to *done* in this construction.

To. As part of an infinitive it should not be separated from the other part by an adverb, as, "to hastily think," for hastily to think, or, to think hastily. Condemnation of the split infinitive is now pretty general, but it is only recently that any one seems to have thought of it. Our forefathers and we elder writers of this generation used it freely and without shame—perhaps because it had not a name, and our crime could not be pointed out without too much explanation.

• • •

As Bierce observes, the split infinitive was used without shame until sometime in the 19th century, though it wasn't used all that often; an increase in its frequency may have been what roused the opposition. Thomas Lounsbury, however, took up the challenge of defending the split infinitive, devoting twenty-six pages of *The Standard of Usage in English* (1908) to the cause. His conclusions are straightforward and still valid: First, "split infinitive" is a misnomer, since *to* is not really part of the infinitive; whether to "split" the construction with an adverb is a stylistic choice. Second, when writers do "split" infinitives, it's generally because the result is more natural English ("I want you to really concentrate"); banning the practice is neither possible nor desirable.

To for At. "We have been to church," "I was to the theater." One can go to a place, but one cannot be to it.

• • •

The complaint about "been to" was new in the 19th century, and Bierce himself had used the expression in an 1873 letter: "Have been to London but once since I wrote you." The critics weren't sure what to think: Fallows 1885 ventured that "been to" was permissible, "because the idea of motion is given." Utter 1916 admitted that "been to" had once been acceptable, but concluded that it was "now vulgar." Josephine Turck Baker banned the usage in *Correct English* (1907), then reversed herself in *The Correct Word* (1920). "It is difficult to avoid the use of *been to*," she said, "for the reason that *been at* or *in* does not seem wholly to convey the meaning." Since that was already the public's opinion, the debate soon fizzled out.

Total. "The figures totaled 10,000." Say, The total of the figures was 10,000.

. . .

Does Bierce mean to condemn the verb *total* altogether, or only when the subject of the verb is *numbers* or *figures*? The latter construction—"the numbers totaled 123"—had only come into use a half century or so earlier. But "He totaled the day's receipts," with a human agent doing the totaling, was two centuries old, and well established. Whatever Bierce's peeve, it was apparently ignored, since *totaled* in both forms was popular. Robert Ransom, in fact, recommended the newer use of the verb, as long as no extra preposition sneaked in: "Various sums when added do not 'total to' a certain amount, but 'total' so much," he instructed in his 1911 newspaper stylebook.

Transaction for **Action,** or **Incident.** "The policeman struck the man with his club, but the transaction was not reported." "The picking of a pocket is a criminal transaction." In a transaction two or more persons must have an active or assenting part; as, a business transaction. Transactions of the Geographical Society, etc. The Society's action would be better called Proceedings.

. . .

"Criminal transaction" is a legal term—"there may be any number of distinct crimes in a single criminal transaction" (*American and English Encyclopedia of Law*, 1898)—and in that use it ignores Bierce's etymologically based claim that the parties must be willing participants. Even in general usage, Webster 1818 and 1913 distinguished between the business sense of *transaction*, which does imply mutual agreement, and the general sense, "the doing or performing of any business." Using *transaction* to report a policeman's clubbing a citizen would surely have constituted journalistic license, but otherwise the use was standard.

As for *proceedings*, perhaps Bierce thought *transaction* had become too commercial to serve as a dignified description of a learned society's activities. But such records had been called transactions since the 17th century, and an outbreak of undignified journalese was not enough to threaten that long tradition.

Transpire for Occur, Happen, etc. "This event transpired in 1906." Transpire (trans, through, and spirare, to breathe) means leak out, that is, become known. What transpired in 1906 may have occurred long before.

· · ·

Transpire has ignored all the stop signs and warning shots directed its way and continued, over the past century, to shift its sense from "leak out" to "happen." The new meaning is not all that farfetched, says *MWDEU*; it probably evolved naturally from the word's ambiguity in sentences like Abigail Adams's "There is nothing new transpired since I wrote you last" (1775).

Though *transpire* was universally condemned in Bierce's time, its status has steadily improved. In the 1960s, only 38 percent of the *American Heritage Dictionary*'s usage panel approved its use for "happen"; in 1998, 58 percent approved; and in 2001, 66 percent. Garner 2003, however, labels this *transpire* "skunked"—too smelly to handle—as well as too pompous for everyday use. But if the newer sense is still on probation, the older one is dying out. In the 2001 *AHD* survey, 48 percent of the usage panel rejected the "become known" sense of *transpire*.

Trifling for Trivial. "A trifling defect"; "a trifling error."

· · ·

Since the participial adjective *trifling* is older than its synonym *trivial*—both date to the 16th century—Bierce probably isn't objecting to *trifling* on grounds of novelty. Most likely it's his passion for order at work once again; if the adjective *trivial* can do the job, why drag in the participle to duplicate its effort? It would be even neater to limit *trifling* to purely verbal uses, as "she's trifling with him." Whatever Bierce's aim, this is his own little fetish; as far as Webster 1913 is concerned, *trifling* and *trivial* are synonyms.

Trust for **Wealthy Corporation.** There are few trusts; capitalists have mostly abandoned the trust form of combination.

• • •

A *trust* was "a combination of commercial or industrial companies, with a central governing body of trustees which holds a majority or the whole of the stock of each of the combining firms, thus having a controlling vote in the conduct and operation of each" (*OED*). Bierce's caution against loose usage is probably aimed at journalists, who sometimes overreach in the quest for linguistic variety. The words have changed, but the idea's the same in today's *Associated Press Stylebook*: "Do not use *firm* in references to an incorporated business entity."

Try an Experiment. An experiment is a trial; we cannot try a trial. Say, make.

• • •

Who first called this expression tautological is unclear, but it seems to have been one of the 19th-century nitpickers. Francis Bacon, in 1625, had used the idiom, writing, "It is good not to try experiments in states" (that is, kinds of government). In an 1860 speech in New York, William Cullen Bryant—he of the *Index Expurgatorius*, the list of words banned in his newsroom—spoke of a time when founding a newspaper was "an experiment that might be tried." Gould 1867 needled Alford 1864 for writing "try the experiment," but Alford, in London, might not have heard of the Americans' animus. And Fitzedward Hall, in the September 1880 issue of the *Nineteenth Century*, pooh-poohed the objection: "The truth is, that there is little or nothing to choose between [*make* and *try*]. *Try an experiment* is almost an instance of what, in Latin grammar, is known as the cognate accusative, of which we have a fair number of samples in older English" (such as *walk the walk, talk the talk, sleep the sleep of the just*).

Hall might have added a practical point: An experiment doesn't always proceed as planned. You may set out to *make* an experiment, but find that you've only *tried* to make it and will have to start over.

Try and for Try to. "I will try and see him." This plainly says that my effort to see him will succeed—which I cannot know and do not wish to affirm. "Please try and come." This colloquial slovenliness of speech is almost universal in this country, but freedom of speech is one of our most precious possessions.

· · ·

Try and remains one of the favorite targets of American peevologists, but it is not, as Bierce believes, an instance of American slovenliness. The usage dates to the 17th century, and it was not always stigmatized. In 1863, just before he published *The Queen's English*, Henry Alford used it in an essay on language: "I really don't wish to be dull; so please, dear reader, to try and not think me so." George Washington Moon, in his counterblast of a book, *The Dean's English,* twitted Alford, calling it "the worst mistake he has made. Try *and* think, indeed!"

The debate hasn't progressed much since then: Some people use *try and*, others say they shouldn't. American critic Robert Palfrey Utter, in *Every-Day Words and Their Uses* (1916), reluctantly conceded that *try and do it* "can be defended as idiomatic—that is, it is very old, and very widespread." But he still pronounced it "always colloquial, and always illogical." H. W. Fowler thought it wasn't worth fussing over: "It is an idiom that should not be discountenanced, but used when it comes natural," he said in *Modern English Usage* (1926). The national division persists today: Garner

2003 calls *try and* a casualism, but he adds that in British English, "*try and* is a standard idiom."

U

Ugly for **Ill-natured, Quarrelsome.** What is ugly is the temper, or disposition, not the person having it.

· · ·

Frank Vizetelly, in *A Desk-Book of Errors* (1906), explained what Bierce is getting at: "*Ugly*, which signifies the reverse of beautiful . . . is colloquially extended in the United States to uncomeliness of character or personal demeanor; as an *ugly* fellow; an *ugly* beast; anger makes him *ugly*. In polite speech this usage is not sanctioned." *Ugly* for "ugly-tempered" seems a reasonable enough shorthand, and it had been used in England more than a century earlier. But once American critics believed it was their own country's invention, they could be counted on to despise it.

Under-handed and **Under-handedly** for **Under-hand.** See *Off-handed.*

· · ·

Several writers, starting with Edward S. Gould in 1867, were shocked at the very existence of *underhanded*. It was superfluous, they said, and besides, in the absence of a verb *to underhand*, there was no legal way to form *underhanded*. The suffix "renders the word a mere vulgarism," wrote Gould.

But the verb *to underhand* was already gestating on cricket pitches and baseball diamonds, where *underhand* was a style of throwing. Today the two adjectives (and adverbs) have more or less divided the lexical territory, with *underhand* (usually) applied to the throw and *underhanded* to sneakiness. "The shorter form is much older," says Garner 2003, "but *underhanded* is now more than twice as common."

Unique. "This is very unique." "The most unique house in the city." There are no degrees of uniqueness: a thing is unique if there is not another like it. The word has nothing to do with oddity, strangeness, nor picturesqueness.

• • •

Bierce's analysis is well known today, but the ban on "very unique" was brand-new when he issued it. *Unique* had only become popular in the mid-19th century, notes *MWDEU*, and its very popularity encouraged the development of extended senses like "unusual" or "rare"—which in turn roused opposition from the strict constructionists.

By now everyone has heard that *unique* should be an "incomparable" word; it's the article of faith that separates the grammatical sheep from the goats. But the rule is widely ignored, and some usage mavens think that's fine. Bergen and Cornelia Evans pointed out half a century ago, in *A Dictionary of Contemporary American Usage*, that *unique* was "merely following the pattern of *singular*" in broadening its use, and there was nothing really wrong with using it to mean "unparalleled" or "remarkable."

The American Heritage Guide to Contemporary Usage (2005) also thinks the issue is overblown. "If *unique* were to be used only according to the strictest criteria of logic," it notes, "it could be applied freely to anything in the world, since nothing is wholly equivalent to anything else. The word *unique*, like many absolute terms, has more than one sense and can be modified with grace in certain uses."

United States as a Singular Noun. "The United States is for peace." The fact that we are in some ways one nation has nothing to do with it; it is enough to know that the word States is plural—if not, what is State? It would be pretty hard on a foreigner skilled in the English tongue if he could not venture to use our national name without having made a study of the history of our Constitution and political institutions. Grammar has not a speaking acquaintance with politics, and patriotic pride is not schoolmaster to syntax.

. . .

United States was a plural noun, as Bierce preferred, when the country was young, but it's usually singular today. The Civil War is often treated as the grammatical turning point, with the Confederates cast as defenders of plurality and the Union fighting for a singular nation. (This version of the story would put Bierce, a Union veteran, on the wrong side of the grammatical divide.) In fact, the change evolved over decades. Abraham Lincoln, in his first inaugural address in 1861, spoke of "the fate of these United States." But James Russell Lowell, writing the same year, used the plural verb even as he rejected the notion of plurality: "The United States are not a German Confederation, but a unitary and indivisible nation."

Bierce's appeal to grammar was no weapon at all, as he must have known; we routinely treat plural forms like *physics*, *measles*, and *news* as singular nouns. By the time Bierce joined the battle, the writing was on the wall for *United States*, and the verb it used was singular.

Unkempt for **Disordered**, **Untidy**, etc. Unkempt means uncombed, and can properly be said of nothing but the hair.

. . .

Tell it to Edmund Spenser: He used the adjective to describe unrefined language in 1579. "To well I wote . . . howe my rymes bene rugged and unkempt" (*OED*). But the 18th century, it's true, used "unkempt" mainly of hair; it was the 19th-century broadening of the "disheveled" sense to rooms, houses, and cornfields that Bierce was (unsuccessfully) protesting.

Use for **Treat**. "The inmates were badly used." "They use him harshly."

• • •

"I suppose the visitor will understand, that he hasn't used me like a gentleman," says a character in Dickens's *Little Dorrit*. We rarely see this *used* anymore except in the term *ill-used*, but it was common from the 16th century to the 18th, according to the *OED*. Wherever Bierce was hearing *used*, it must have sounded old-fashioned by the early 20th century.

Utter for **Absolute, Entire**, etc. Utter has a damnatory signification and is to be used of evil things only. It is correct to say utter misery, but not "utter happiness"; utterly bad, but not "utterly good."

• • •

Apparently Bierce borrowed a mild version of this "rule" from Alfred Ayres and kicked it up a notch or three. Ayres, in *The Verbalist* (1881), had said that because *utter* was negative, "utter concord" was an impossible expression. They were both overstating the case; while *utter* does have a certain affinity for the negative, it has never been reserved for "evil things only." The *OED* has 15th-century examples of "utterly free" and "utterly fair," and Bierce's fellow commentators, like the rest of us, used *utterly* to modify words like *different*, *distinct*, *finished*, and *astonished*. Bierce's rule is, to borrow a phrase from Shaw, utter bosh.

V

Various for **Several**. "Various kinds of men." Kinds are various of course, for they vary—that is what makes them kinds. Use various only when, in speaking of a number of things, you wish to direct attention to their variety—their difference, one from another. "The dividend was distributed among the various stockholders." The stockholders vary, as do all persons, but that is irrelevant and was not in mind. "Various persons have spoken to me of you." Their variation is unimportant; what is meant is that there was a small indefinite number of them; that is, several.

• • •

Even Bierce's fellow usage mavens might have responded to this with "Get a life, Ambrose." This "weakened sense" of *various*, merging into "different," dates to 1695, says the *OED*; if most people are ignoring the fine distinctions Bierce sees, it's because most people no longer notice them.

Ventilate for **Express, Disclose**, etc. "The statesman ventilated his views." A disagreeable and dog-eared figure of speech.

• • •

"While we may say that a man airs his notions at a public meeting or in a newspaper," wrote White 1870, "I am not prepared to defend the good taste of saying that he ventilates them. But this use of *ventilate* is not a neologism." Nor was it: The *OED*'s first example, in which *ventilate* means "discuss," dates to 1527.* The word was frequent in the 17th century, fell out of use, then returned in the mid-19th century. Familiarity bred contempt; once *ventilate* was back in vogue, it was attacked as slang or political jargon. In 1871 Disraeli called it "a barbarous expression." And Schele de Vere 1872 criticized the *New York Herald*'s "abuse" of the term in using it of a person, when the paper promised "to ventilate the President and his policy." The verb didn't die off soon enough for Bierce: In Webster 1913, "to expose to examination and discussion" was still a standard sense of *ventilate*.

---

* Today's verb *vent*—"I need to vent about my boss"—is not a clipped form of *ventilate*; it has been a separate word since the early 1600s, used not of facts and opinions (which were *ventilated*) but of emotions.

Verbal for **Oral**. All language is verbal, whether spoken or written, but audible speech is oral. "He did not write, but communicated his wishes verbally." It would have been a verbal communication, also, if written.

. . .

People had been using *verbal* to mean "oral" for two hundred years, without confusing anyone, before William Hodgson, in 1881, made the etymological point Bierce repeats, that "verbal" applies to all words. Johnson's *Dictionary* (1755), as well as Webster 1828 and 1913, listed the first sense of *verbal* as "spoken, not written." Schele de Vere, a professor of modern languages at the University of Virginia, used *verbal* for "oral" in *Americanisms* (1871): "The contract is binding, as far as verbal agreements have any force." And *MWDEU* has a long list of respected writers who used *verbal* for *oral*, including Pepys, Swift, Fielding, Trollope, and Dickens.

But Hodgson, Bierce, and their collaborators created a monster. Their shibboleth—the lawyerly distinction between *verbal* and *oral*—is still heard today, though it's still widely ignored. In *Every-Day Words and Their Uses* (1916), Robert Palfrey Utter recognized the "strict" usage recommendation—then only twenty-five years old—but correctly described the reality. "In common parlance *oral* and *verbal* mean the same thing."

Vest for **Waistcoat**. This is American, but as all Americans are not in agreement* about it it is better to use the English word.

. . .

Other commentators suggest that Americans were, in fact, pretty much in agreement about *vest*. Bartlett 1848 said of his fellow Americans, "We almost always use this word instead of *waistcoat*,

---

* Bierce is strict on the placement of *only*, but apparently he hasn't yet extended the rule to cover the placement of *not*. Many a modern editor would correct his phrasing here to "not all Americans are in agreement."

which we rarely apply to anything but an under garment." Schele de Vere 1871 said, "*Vest* is in America almost universally used for the English waistcoat, while the latter is very appropriately applied to a garment worn immediately on the body." Bierce may have been affected by memories of his years in England, but he was behind the times. The senses of *vest* and *waistcoat* were splitting, and the British ended up with *vest* meaning "undershirt" and with *waistcoat* for what we call a *vest*.

Vicinity for **Vicinage**, or **Neighborhood**. "He lives in this vicinity." If neither of the other words is desired say, He lives in the vicinity of this place, or, better, He lives near by.

· · ·

This is Bierce at his most vexatious. Nobody else wanted to ban the phrase "in this vicinity" or resurrect the word *vicinage*; for other commentators, the problem was "Washington and vicinity," the short form of "Washington and *its* vicinity." This was just as bad, the critics said, as saying "Washington and neighborhood." Since *neighborhood* and *vicinity* are used differently today, and *vicinage* survives only in legal usage, we can safely ignore the question.

View of. "He invested with the view of immediate profit." "He enlisted with the view of promotion." Say, with a view to.

· · ·

We do say "with a view to," when we use the phrase at all, and if there were once dissenters from the Rule of the One True Preposition, they have left few traces.

Vulgar for **Immodest, Indecent.** It is from vulgus, the common people, the mob, and means both common and unrefined, but has no relation to indecency.

· · ·

The high-minded language critics hoped to keep *vulgar* well clear of sexual connotations, but the word had been on the slippery slope since the 17th century. "From its frequent qualification of the conduct and the speech of the vulgar, [the word] came in natural course, to mean low, rude, impolite," said Richard Grant White (*Words and Their Uses*, 1870). And once the word meant "low" and "rude" speech, how to prevent it from being applied to other practices of the low and rude?

White insisted that *vulgar* shouldn't be used to mean "immodest," providing a cautionary example: "A lady not without culture said to another of a third, 'She dresses very low; but as she has no figure, it doesn't look vulgar;' meaning, by the feminine malice of her apology, that it did not look immodest." White thought the "lady" was misusing the word, but if excessive cleavage was considered a "common" sort of display, it seems natural that *vulgar* would be used to disparage it. And Ayres 1881 made it clear that the change was well under way: "By the many, this word is probably more frequently used improperly than properly," he said. In other words, the majority had already decided that *vulgar* could indeed mean "immodest."

W

Way for Away. "Way out at sea." "Way down South."

• • •

"*Way* or '*way*, as an abbreviation of the adverb *away*, as ''*way* out West,' is an impropriety of speech," said Vizetelly 1906. "Say, rather, "He has gone (or is in the) West." The shortened *away* was nothing new—the *OED* shows it in use as early as 1205—but it was only in the 19th century that it came to mean "far, a distance," and met with disapproval. Today it is standard but, says *AHD4*, "has an informal ring."

Ways for **Way.** "A squirrel ran a little ways along the road." "The ship looked a long ways off." This surprising word calls loudly for depluralization.

. . .

Ways has been used for *way* in expressions like "a ways up the street" since the 16th century, but it still surprises critics: Garner 2003 says that because the word is dialectal, it's "surprising to find [it] in serious journalism." Not everyone agrees with his label: *AHD4* calls *ways* acceptable but informal, and *MWDEU* says it's standard American English. The final *s* may have stuck because it's useful, especially in speech, for distinguishing *a ways*—meaning "a distance"—from the many other senses of *way*. Without it, how would we understand "It's still a ways away"?

Wed for **Wedded.** "They were wed at noon." "He wed her in Boston." The word wed in all its forms as a substitute for marry, is pretty hard to bear.

. . .

Bierce, in the guise of the Melancholy Author, had addressed *wed* more colorfully in an earlier newspaper article, reprinted in the *Writer*: "The man who in cold prose, and himself cold sober, will write the word 'wed,' in any of its moods and tenses, is an immortal ass." *Wed* and *wedded* may have sounded stilted even in Bierce's day, but journalistic convenience, if nothing else, has kept them in use. The irregular past—"They wed yesterday"—was dialectal in 1909, but both *wed* and *wedded* are now standard for both past and past participle.

Well. As a mere meaningless prelude to a sentence this word is overtasked. "Well, I don't know about that." "Well, you may try." "Well, have your own way."

. . .

Every age has its own meaningless preludes (and interludes, and postludes); know what I mean? They are generally restricted to spoken English, and like the weather or hemlines, they're unpredictable and sometimes irresistible. As Bierce should know: In this very book, in the entry for *locate*, he writes, "well, dictionaries are funny."

Wet for Wetted. See *Bet.*

· · ·

Wet is another of the verbs—like *bet*, *wed*, *quit*—that Bierce thought should stick to a regular past tense. Even today, though *wet* is the favored form, the past tense can go either way.

Where for When. "Where there is reason to expect criticism write discreetly."

· · ·

Bierce's literalism surfaces again—apparently he thinks it is wrong to use *where* of a situation rather than a place. He fails to notice that *when*, in this case, is just as figurative as *where*; it no more refers to a literal time than *where* does to place. Either word, in this usage, means something like "in a situation in which." Scott and Denney were among the many language mavens to use the construction: "According to some authorities, the noun *alternative* can be used only where there is a choice between two things," they wrote in *Elementary English Composition* (1900). *When* has been used this way since the 12th century, *where* since the 14th, and both are unimpeachable English.

Which for That. "The boat which I engaged had a hole in it." But a parenthetical clause may rightly be introduced by which; as, The boat, which had a hole in it, I nevertheless engaged. Which and that are seldom interchangeable; when they are, use that. It sounds better.

· · ·

Bierce is here endorsing the *which-that* rule, which was just emerging into usage consciousness in his day. According to this now ubiquitous American superstition, *which* is only properly used in a nonrestrictive clause, with commas setting it off: "Her shoes, which looked expensive, were ruined." It would be wrong, according to this theory, to write, "The shoes which I bought were vastly overpriced." Only *that* would be proper in this clause.

The "rule" had been suggested as early as 1806, and Bierce may have seen a detailed discussion of it in Alfred Ayres's *The Verbalist* (1881); Ayres had reprinted the entire *which-that* section from Alexander Bain's 1863 *English Grammar*. Bierce, who was surely the kind of kid who never let his peas touch his mashed potatoes, naturally welcomed the new distinction.

But even among usage writers, the word spread slowly. When Fowler 1926 restated the rule, it was as a preference: "There would be much to gain both in lucidity & in ease," he said, if people would restrict the pronouns to separate uses. But he admitted that "it would be idle to pretend that this is the practice either of most or of the best writers."

In the United States, there was skepticism as late as the mid-20th century. Evans and Evans 1957, responding to Fowler, said, "What is not the practice of most, or of the best, is not part of our language." But only two years later, Strunk and White's *Elements of Style* bulldozed over the Evanses' doubts and began laying down the *which-that* law in earnest. (Ironically, Strunk himself didn't follow the rule; it was foisted on him posthumously by his coauthor, who revised Strunk's original 1918 text to replace errant *which*es with *that*s.)

How do we observe the rule now? *MWDEU* sums it up: Virtually nobody uses *that* instead of *which* in nonrestrictive clauses (though the use was once common—as in Richard Grant White's "dictionaries of the present day, that swell every few years by a thousand items"). But we still find *which* in restrictive clauses:

"Mrs. Little . . . weighed him on a small scale which was really meant for weighing letters." E. B. White said that such use of *which* was incorrect, but the sentence, from *Stuart Little*, is his own.

In fact, says *MWDEU*, usage "has pretty much settled down. You can use either *which* or *that* to introduce a restrictive clause— the grounds for your choice should be stylistic—and *which* to introduce a nonrestrictive clause." If E. B. White could ignore his own rule, surely the rest of us can too.

Whip for **Chastise**, or **Defeat**. To whip is to beat with a whip. It means nothing else.

• • •

Hates polysemy, it's weedy and rank, that's why the satirist is a crank . . . Of course *whip* had other senses besides "beat with a whip." *Whip* meant "move quickly," as in "he whipped out a knife." It meant to beat egg whites, to make a spinning top go, to make a certain fencing move, and more. What Bierce wants to condemn, most likely, is *whip* meaning "defeat." The use had been first recorded in 1571, but by Bierce's day it was considered an American colloquialism, and no wonder: Davy Crockett's boast, "I can whip my weight in wildcats," was known from sea to shining sea. That avowal, it's safe to say, would have sounded to Bierce like the crudest of backwoods bombast.

Whiskers for **Beard**. The whisker is that part of the beard that grows on the cheek. See *Chin Whiskers*.

• • •

Both in England and in America, facial hair fashions—and the words to designate them—were in flux. The *OED* quotes an 1823 English dialect survey on the changes in this one: "Whiskers [means] the hair on the upper lip, as until lately, I believe, [it did] all over England. Now, the hair under the ears, sometimes under the eyes also, bear[s] this term, and the labial comæ, are called moustaches." See *Goatee, Sideburns*.

Who for **Whom.** "Who do you take me for?"

• • •

Who was used for *whom* in some constructions, including the one Bierce objects to, as early as the 14th century—just as it is today. "In many contexts, *whom* sounds forced or pretentiously correct," says the *American Heritage Guide to Contemporary Usage* (2005). It must have sounded forced to Thomas Cranmer, archbishop of Canterbury, when he wrote to Henry VIII in 1540 of an adviser arrested for treason: "Who shall your grace trust hereafter, if you might not trust him?" *Whom* is not yet extinct, but in sentence-initial position it is well on its way to oblivion.

Whom for **Who.** "The man whom they thought was dead is living." Here the needless introduction of was entails the alteration of whom to who. "Remember whom it is that you speak of." Who and whom trip up many a good writer, although, unlike which and who, they require nothing but knowledge of grammar.

• • •

Whom and *who* can be hard to untangle in the midst of a complicated construction. But the mistake was abroad, says *MWDEU*, before anyone had called it a mistake; expressions like "remember whom it is" cropped up before Robert Lowth, in 1763, had issued a rule on the matter. And this *whom* situation is not getting worse, says *MWDEU*. As with *who* for *whom*, the variations today "are in kind just about the same as they were in Shakespeare's day." See *Than Whom*.

Widow Woman. Omit woman.

• • •

Various other language writers inveighed against *widow woman*, but the expression—perhaps rooted in Irish—was dialectal or regional in both Britain and America. It appeared in fiction reproducing colloquial speech, but there's no evidence that it ever threatened to make its way into standard usage.

Will and **Shall**. Proficiency in the use of these apparently troublesome words must be sought in text-books on grammar and rhetoric, where the subject will be found treated with a more particular attention, and at greater length, than is possible in a book of the character of this. Briefly and generally, in the first person, a mere intention is indicated by shall, as, I shall go; whereas will denotes some degree of compliance or determination, as, I will go—as if my going had been requested or forbidden. In the second and the third person, will merely forecasts, as, You (or he) will go; but shall implies something of promise, permission or compulsion by the speaker, as, You (or he) shall go. Another and less obvious compulsion—that of circumstance—speaks in shall, as sometimes used with good effect: In Germany you shall not turn over a chip without uncovering a philosopher. The sentence is barely more than indicative, shall being almost, but not quite, equivalent to can.

· · ·

The classic illustration of the use of *will* and *shall* is an anecdote, dating to at least 1800, in which a Frenchman (or other non-native speaker of English) falls overboard. Sadly, he doesn't know *will* from *shall*. He shouts, "I will drown, and no one shall save me!"— little knowing that in proper English this means "I am determined to drown, and no one will be allowed to save me." His only chance of rescue is to cry out, "I shall drown, and no one will save me!"— a dire prediction, not a statement of intention. (Of course, he should be shouting, "Help!"—but that would ruin the story.)

Some usage writers still mention *shall* and *will*, for old times' sake, but Wilson Follett's twenty-page excursus on the subject, in *Modern American Usage* (1966), seems to have killed American enthusiasm for the distinction once and for all.

Win for **Won.** "I went to the race and win ten dollars." This atrocious solecism seems to be unknown outside the world of sport, where may it ever remain.

* * *

"I win ten dollars" no longer plagues listeners, but sports lingo springs eternal. If Bierce were still with us, he'd be joining the chorus of complaints about announcers who narrate past events in the present tense: "If he catches the ball here, the Sox win."

Win out. Like its antithesis, "lose out," this reasonless phrase is of sport, "sporty."

* * *

Most critics think of such phrasal verbs—those with allegedly superfluous prepositions—as Americanisms, not sportsisms. Even now, the BBC's style guide lists *free up, consult with, win out, and check up on* as Americanisms, "not yet standard English." But as Garner 2003 concedes, there are instances—*face up to, lose out,* and (presumably) Bierce's *win out*—where the prepositions do "add a nuance to the verb."

Without for **Unless.** "I cannot go without I recover." Peasantese.

* * *

This *without* was once respectable, says the *OED*—it appears in Shakespeare—but by the 18th century it was colloquial, and by the 19th it was beginning to sound uneducated. "Almost everybody uses this word as the synonyme of *unless,*" said Gould 1867, "but such a use of the word is entirely unjustifiable." Gould may have spoken too soon—and too sweepingly—but when the

Evanses said, in 1957, that the usage was "no longer considered standard," they were on firmer ground.

Witness for See. To witness is more than merely to see, or observe; it is to observe, and to tell afterward.

. . .

Witness does mean more than *see*—it means to see or experience something, usually an event or occurrence, firsthand. We *witness* a plane crash; we *see* a televised car chase or the Grand Canyon. But Bierce's idea, that you haven't witnessed until you've spoken, is a 19th-century misconception; the *OED* has examples of *witness* meaning simply "see firsthand," with no testifying implied, dating to the 16th century. Perhaps *witness* is sometimes used as "a big synonyme of see," as White 1870 believed, but whether it's too big a synonym, in any given instance, readers can decide for themselves.

Would-be. "The would-be assassin was arrested." The word doubtless supplies a want, but we can better endure the want than the word. In the instance of the assassin, it is needless, for he who attempts to murder is an assassin, whether he succeeds or not.

. . .

No doubt *would-be* seems cobbled together and inelegant to Bierce, but it's good English. Literature since the 17th century, as Bierce must have noticed, has been well populated with would-be philosophers, wits, beaux, and, yes, assassins. So maybe his real motive here is to nitpick about *assassin*.

Bierce is correct that *assassin* applies to both successful and unsuccessful killers; a sentence like "His assassin waited in the shadows" doesn't necessariy need a *would-be*. But the writer who in 1889 referred to "Cantillon, the would-be assassin of Wellington," was wise to use the *would-be*; to call the man simply "the assassin of Wellington" might have startled even readers who knew Wellington had not been murdered. And today, Bierce's naked *assassin* is increasingly rare. Since *assassinated* means "killed," we find it more natural—and less confusing—to use *assassin* not for a plotter or an assailant, but only for a successful killer.

ACKNOWLEDGMENTS

This exploration of century-old language peeves is not meant to plumb the depths of usage history; it's more backyard treasure hunt than deep-sea salvage operation. But I couldn't have gone even this far without the scholars, linguists, and lexicographers who helped me learn to read the pirate map.

Every aspiring usage maven owes a debt to the matchless Language Log blog and the linguists who instruct and entertain us there. Arnold Zwicky, Geoffrey Nunberg, Ben Zimmer, Geoffrey Pullum, and Mark Liberman have been especially helpful in my continuing education. Steven Pinker, Jesse Sheidlower, and Erin McKean are always there when I need them. Thanks, too, to the readers of my *Boston Globe* column, "The Word," for a dozen years' worth of thought-provoking (and occasionally just provoking) queries.

Closer to home, my personal editing posse—Laura Shapiro, Diane McWhorter, Betsy Meyer, Louise Kennedy, and Vicki Croke—volunteered their sharp eyes and sharper wits to the project. I'm also grateful to my family, near and far, and especially to my husband, Paul Solman, who kept me well supplied with coffee and merriment.

BIBLIOGRAPHY

This is not a complete list of works cited, but includes books that were especially useful, as well as a couple that are cited just once but are too interesting to omit. The pre-1920 books were consulted at Google Books or other online sites (as noted), where their searchability is a great boon for research of this kind; thumbing through the paper editions would have been a great but very prolonged pleasure. With the entries for these earlier, less familiar authors, I've included a few biographical details.

ABBREVIATIONS

AHD4   *American Heritage Dictionary of the English Language*.
2000. 4th ed. Boston: Houghton Mifflin.
MWDEU   *Merriam-Webster's Dictionary of English Usage*. 1994.
Springfield, Mass.: Merriam-Webster.
OED   *Oxford English Dictionary Online*. Oxford University
Press. http://dictionary.oed.com.

Alford, Henry. 1864. *The Queen's English: Stray Notes on Speaking and Spelling*. London: Strahan. Alford (1810–1871) was educated at Cambridge University and later taught there. He was also a poet, student of English idiom, and Anglican priest; he became dean of Canterbury Cathedral in 1857, and is often referred to as Dean Alford. (A rebuttal to his book, by George Washington Moon, was titled *The Dean's English*.)

The American Heritage Guide to Contemporary Usage and Style. 2005. Boston: Houghton Mifflin.

Ayres, Alfred. 1881, 2nd ed. 1896. *The Verbalist: A Manual Devoted to Brief Discussions of the Right and the Wrong Use of Words*. New

York: D. Appleton. Ayres was the pen name of Thomas Embly Osmun (1826–1902), an American critic and elocutionist whose day job in New York was working with stage actors on pronunciation and voice technique.

Bache, Richard Meade. 1869. *Vulgarisms & Other Errors of Speech*. 2nd ed. Philadelphia: Claxton, Remsen and Haffelfinger. Bache (1830–1907), a descendant of Benjamin Franklin, also wrote a biography of his uncle, the Civil War general George Gordon Meade.

Bain, Alexander. 1863. *An English Grammar*. London: Longmans, Green. A Scottish mathematician and philosopher, Bain (1818–1903) wrote his grammar as part of his effort to improve education in Scotland.

Baker, Josephine Turck. 1907. *Correct English: How to Use It*. Baltimore: Sadler-Rowe.

———. 1920. *The Correct Word: How to Use It: A Complete Alphabetic List*. Chicago: Correct English Publishing. Baker was founding editor of *Correct English*, a monthly magazine published in Chicago from 1899 into the 1940s, and author of a number of popular usage, grammar, and vocabulary books.

Baker, Robert. 1770. *Remarks on the English Language*. London: J. Bell. Little is known about Baker, who published this collection of usage tips anonymously, except that he trusted his own judgment.

Bartlett, John Russell. 1848. *Dictionary of Americanisms*. New York: Bartlett & Welford. 4th ed. 1877. Boston: Little, Brown. Bartlett (1805–1886) was a Providence businessman with little formal education, but a love of literature and publishing, who wrote a total of nineteen books.

Bernstein, Theodore M. 1965. *The Careful Writer*. New York: Atheneum.

———. 1971. *Miss Thistlebottom's Hobgoblins*. New York: Farrar, Straus and Giroux.

Bierce, Ambrose. 2000. *The Unabridged Devil's Dictionary*. Ed. David E. Schultz and S. T. Joshi. Athens: University of Georgia Press.

Breen, Henry H. 1857. *Modern English Literature: Its Blemishes and Defects*. London: Longman, Brown. Born in Ireland, Breen (1805–

1882) published accounts of his life as a civil administrator in the West Indies as well as poetry and language criticism.

Brown, Goold. 1851. *The Grammar of English Grammars*. New York: Samuel S. and William Wood. Brown (1791–1857) was a New Englander who taught school in Rhode Island and in New York City. *The Cambridge History of the English Language* calls his book "the densest English grammar of the nineteenth century, a colossus."

Bryant, William Cullen. 1870. *Index Expurgatorius*. Reprinted in Bernstein 1971. Bryant (1794–1878), the well-known poet who wrote "To a Waterfowl" and "Thanatopsis," was editor of the *New York Evening Post* for nearly fifty years. His *Index*, a list of words not to be used in the newspaper, was not formally published; I've dated it 1870 because the earliest mention of it I've found is in the January 1871 *British Quarterly Review*.

Burgess, Walton. 1855. *Five Hundred Mistakes of Daily Occurrence . . . Corrected*. New York: Daniel Burgess. According to a *New York Times* obituary, Walton Burgess had worked for his father's publishing business in New York City, then started his own. He "dropped dead of paralysis" in his office, aged fifty-seven, in December 1890.

The Columbia Guide to Standard American English. 1993. Ed. Kenneth G. Wilson. New York: Columbia University Press.

Crabb, George. 1818. *English Synonymes Explained*. 2nd ed. London: Baldwin, Cradock. Crabb (1778–1851) began to study medicine, but "quit the field after fainting during dissections," says Joshua Kendall in *The Man Who Made Lists*, his 2008 Roget biography. Crabb's synonym book, in that pre-Roget era, went into sixteen editions.

Evans, Bergen, and Cornelia Evans. 1957. *A Dictionary of Contemporary American Usage*. New York: Random House.

Fallows, Samuel. 1885. *Discriminate*. New York: D. Appleton. Fallows (1835–1922) was born in England but brought up in Wisconsin; he became a pastor, educator, officer in the Civil War, writer, and eventually bishop of the Reformed Episcopal Church.

Fitzgerald, Joseph. 1901. *Word and Phrase: True and False Use in English*. New York: A. C. McClurg. Fitzgerald explains in his preface that his "practical manual" treats words that "suggested themselves to the author during the years that he was assistant editor of the *North American Review* and the *Forum*, specially the latter."

Follett, Wilson. 1966. *Modern American Usage*. New York: Hill and Wang.

Fowler, Henry Watson. 1906. *The King's English*. Oxford: Clarendon Press.

———. 1926. *A Dictionary of Modern English Usage*. Oxford: Oxford University Press.

Garner, Bryan A. 2003. *Garner's Modern American Usage*. 2nd ed. New York: Oxford University Press.

Gould, Edward S. 1867. *Good English*. New York: W. J. Widdleton. Gould (1808–1885) was a New York merchant, critic, writer, and playwright; his book, like Moon's, was an attack on *The Queen's English*.

Hall, Fitzedward. 1872. *Recent Exemplifications of False Philology*. New York: Scribner, Armstrong.

———. *Modern English*. 1873. New York: Scribner, Armstrong. Hall (1825–1901) was born in western New York and educated at Rensselaer Polytechnic and Harvard, and taught Sanskrit and English in India. Moving to London, he taught at King's College, then retired to private philology; he was a significant contributor to the *Oxford English Dictionary*, then in its early stages.

Hall, J. Lesslie. 1917. *English Usage*. New York: Scott, Foresman. Hall (1856–1928), a professor at William and Mary for forty years, also wrote an Anglo-Saxon grammar and translated *Beowulf* and other Old English poetry.

Hodgson, William B. 1881. *Errors in the Use of English*. Edinburgh: David Douglas. Hodgson (1815–1880), born in Edinburgh, was an education reformer and professor of economics at the University of Edinburgh.

Hurd, Seth T. 1847. *A Grammatical Corrector*. Philadelphia: E. H. Butler. "The famous lecturer on English grammar" (as one periodical called him) was also a lawyer and editor of the *Brownsville* (Pa.) *Clipper*.

Lounsbury, Thomas R. 1908. *The Standard of Usage in English*. New

York: Harper & Brothers. Lounsbury (1838–1915) was among the first scholars to delve into the history of usage and of attitudes toward it. He was a professor of English at Yale and a member of the simplified spelling movement.

Lowth, Robert. 1763. *A Short Introduction to English Grammar*. 2nd ed. London: A. Millar and R. and J. Dodsley. A Bible scholar and translator, professor of poetry at Oxford, and bishop of London, Lowth (1710–1787) was founding father of the prescriptivist tradition.

Mathews, William. 1876. *Words; Their Use and Abuse*. Chicago: S. C. Griggs. Mathews (1818–1909) was a lawyer, publisher, and University of Chicago professor, and finally a successful Boston-based author.

Moon, George Washington. 1865. *The Dean's English*. 4th ed. London: Hatchard. Moon, a London poet and writer whose parents were Americans, is remembered mainly for his battle of the books with Dean Henry Alford, which lasted through several editions on both sides.

Morris, Roy, Jr. 1996. *Ambrose Bierce: Alone in Bad Company*. New York: Crown.

Murray, Lindley. 1809. *An English Grammar, Adapted to the Different Classes of Learners*. 16th ed. Philadelphia: Benjamin Johnson. A New York businessman who moved to England in midlife, Murray (1745–1826) there became a writer, and his grammar was a huge bestseller on both sides of the Atlantic.

O'Connor, Richard. 1967. *Ambrose Bierce: A Biography*. Boston: Little, Brown.

Partridge, Eric. 1954. *The Concise Usage and Abusage*. London: H. Hamilton.

Piozzi, Hester Lynch. 1794. *British Synonymy*. London: G. G. and J. Robinson. As Mrs. Thrale, Piozzi (1741–1821), herself a writer, was Samuel Johnson's constant companion in London. Once widowed, she shocked society by marrying an Italian music teacher, but continued to write and publish.

Ransom, Robert W. 1911. *Hints & "Don'ts" for Writers and Copyreaders*. Chicago: Chicago Record-Herald. Ransom was an editor at the *Chicago Record-Herald*.

Raub, Albert Newton. 1897. *Helps in the Use of Good English*. Philadelphia: Raub. A Pennsylvania native, Raub (1840–1904) was a public school administrator, lecturer, and writer and publisher of school textbooks who also served as president of Delaware College.

Schele de Vere, Maximilian. 1871. *Americanisms: The English of the New World*. New York: Charles Scribner. Schele de Vere (1820–1898), a native of Sweden with a Ph.D. from Berlin, was a professor of modern languages at the University of Virginia.

Scott, Fred Newton, and Joseph Villiers Denney. 1900. *Elementary English Composition*. Boston: Allyn & Bacon. Scott, a professor of rhetoric at the University of Michigan, and Denney, his counterpart at Ohio State University, collaborated on a number of books about the teaching of writing.

Smith, Charles John. 1864. *Synonyms Discriminated*. New York: Henry Holt. Educated at Oxford, Smith (1818–1872) was vicar of a parish in Kent and archdeacon of Jamaica.

Trench, Richard Chenevix. 1852. *On the Study of Words*. 2nd ed. Clinton Hall, N.Y.: Redfield.

———. 1855. *English Past and Present*. New York: Redfield. Trench (1807–1886), a poet and philologist educated at Cambridge, was an Anglican clergyman and eventually archbishop of Dublin, as well as one of the founders of the *Oxford English Dictionary*.

Tucker, Gilbert M. 1895. *Our Common Speech*. New York: Dodd, Mead. Educated at Williams College, Tucker (1847–1932) succeeded his father as editor and publisher of *Country Gentleman*, in Albany, and also published in literary journals.

Utter, Robert Palfrey. 1916. *Every-Day Words and Their Uses*. New York: Harper & Brothers. Utter (1875–1936) graduated from Harvard and was a longtime professor of English at the University of California at Berkeley.

Vizetelly, Frank. 1906. *A Desk-Book of Errors in English*. New York: Funk & Wagnalls. Vizetelly (1864–1938), born in London, came to New York in his twenties and worked his way up at the publisher Funk & Wagnalls till he was editor of the *Standard Dictionary*; for thirty years he wrote a popular language column in *Literary Digest*.

Webster, Noah. 1828. *American Dictionary of the English Language*. (Accessed at the University of Chicago's ARTFL Project: http://machaut.uchicago.edu.)

———. 1913. *Webster's Revised Unabridged Dictionary of the English Language*. Springfield, Mass.: G. & C. Merriam. (Accessed at http://machaut.uchicago.edu.)

White, Richard Grant. 1870. *Words and Their Uses, Past and Present*. New York: Sheldon. White (1822–1885), a lifelong New Yorker, was a nonpracticing lawyer, a journalist, a Shakespeare scholar, a cellist, and the father of architect Stanford White.

A NOTE ON THE AUTHORS

In *The Devil's Dictionary*, AMBROSE BIERCE (1842–1914?),
defined *cynic* as "a blackguard whose faulty vision
sees things as they are, not as they ought to be"—a
description he strove to embody throughout his long and
witty career. His writing includes journalism, poetry, satire,
and fiction, much of it based on his Civil War experience.
In 1913 he set off for Mexico, then in the throes of
revolution, and was never seen again.

• • •

JAN FREEMAN has been writing the *Boston Sunday Globe*'s
weekly language column, "The Word," since 1997.
A lifelong usage geek with a graduate degree in English, she
has worked as an editor at the *Real Paper*,
Boston magazine, *Inc.* magazine, and the *Boston Globe*.
She lives in Newton, Massachusetts.